THE ULTIMATE BRAAI MASTER:

ROAD
tripping

-WITH-

JUSTIN BONELLO

WRITTEN BY HELENA LOMBARD

First published by Penguin Random House South Africa (Pty) Ltd
Company Reg. No. 1953/000441/07

The Estuaries No. 4, Oxbow Crescent, Century Avenue, Century City 7441
PO Box 1144, Cape Town 8000, South Africa

www.penguinbooks.co.za

ISBN 978-1-41520-876-2

Written by Justin Bonello and Helena Lombard
Photography by Louis Hiemstra, Daniela Zondagh and Sunel Haasbroek
Food styling by Caro Gardner
Design and layout by twoshoes.co.za
Printed and bound by Toppan Leefung Packaging and Printing (Dongguan) Co. Ltd, China

Contents

In memory of
Kai Auchincloss

This book is dedicated to my late and dear friend Kai. Sometimes in our journeys we meet kindred spirits who are as we are, who become friends that we'd like to carry for the rest of our lives – a late dear friend of mine once said to me that we're lucky if we can count on our hands those who we consider good friends... And Kai, you were one of those who I counted.

You'll always be in my mind and heart. RIP.

FOREWORD

How do you survive almost 9 000 kilometres of travelling dirt roads? Nine thousand kilometres of new adventures, misadventures, old friends, new friends, badly behaved friends? What does it take to be away from all your creature comforts for two months? For 70 days and the 1 400-odd hours that fly by in a moment?

We like to think it takes a very special breed of human. The dust-kickers, crazy hearts and adrenalin seekers. The runaways. The hippies-in-the-making. The accidentals and the newbies. The type of people who suit-and-tie-wearing-9-to-5-ers are secretly envious of. Those who celebrate new friendships in endless car rides, with endless playlists. Those who talk around blazing fires late into the night and early hours of the morning. The ones who do impromptu *langarm* dancing and drink disgusting shooters in another dodgy bar and in another nameless small town all in the name of sanity. The type of people who can get up at stupid-o-clock and graft hard (*really* hard) for 15 hours straight, party for six and sleep for only three. Then do it all over again the next day.

Being on the road is a place where time becomes an afterthought – something that is laughed at because, after a while, you no longer know what day of the week it is, because, let's face it, out here, it doesn't really matter. The only things that matter are the sunsets and sunrises, and how we try to steal time because sleeping feels like a waste.

This is where we all lose our heads a little. Some of us lose our hearts and others find them. Where we all gain new perspectives and some discover new directions. But we celebrate this.

We feel alive when it becomes so quiet at night that we get back into touch with every sense of who we are. Life on the road is not reality. It's a many days, many weeks, many months dreamscape where we create our own version of what is real, and recreate ourselves.

Being on the road and doing the work that goes into filming a 13-part reality TV series is not for just anyone and it's definitely not for the faint at heart. But in a sense it is no different to a large group of friends who live and travel together for a while. In our industry, it's for the lucky, crazy few. For some of us, and after long enough, returning home to our family, dogs, chores, responsibilities and to our people is celebrated.

But never for too long. After a couple of weeks of enjoying those man-made creature comforts and having the quiet of the wild replaced with the quiet of the city, the itch starts. It's the familiar burn to get in your car and drive into a landscape where there are no fences and no rules. This is the curse of the traveller and the life of a road tripper. And we embrace it with arms wide open every time we get to pack up and set out on a new adventure.

This is your invitation to get in your car and take a ride with us. But fasten your seatbelts. It gets a little bumpy.

BUT
before you go...

We've been on enough road trips to know what to pack and what to toss out the car last minute. Use this as a guideline for what to have in your car for *every and any* road trip you're going on.

1. Passport and Driver's Licence. Make sure these are valid and not from 19-*voetsek*! You'll be really bummed if you get to a border and you've either forgotten to pack your passport or the one you have was the one you got when you were planning a trip overseas in an act of rebellion back in varsity. And you definitely don't need a traffic fine from a smug-looking *spietkop* because your driver's licence has expired. These things can ruin a road trip! On that note, if you're going to cross the border, take some copies of both to hand out to trigger-happy traffic cops that are looking to get a buck out of you.

2. Decent Music – and lots of it! Check out page 18 for one of our road tripping playlists, and make it one of yours!

3. A Pillow. If you're planning on driving for more than six hours, which we often do, it's a good idea to have a road trip buddy and to take turns driving. The pillow is for the passenger... not the driver, should they want to have a little impromptu nap – it might as well be comfortable. A good pillow is especially handy if you're going to go camping.

4. Layers. Long pants. Short pants. T-shirts. Sweatshirts. Hats. Beanies. Swimwear. Gloves. Underwear. All terrain shoes, or hiking boots. Flip-flops. Raincoat. Socks. (You don't need five of each – except maybe for underwear and socks – if you do, you're doing it wrong and you'll drag along a lot of things that will never see the light of day.) In short, pack stuff that will prepare you for all kinds of weather.

5. Cooking Utensils. Should you decide to go camping then these sure come in handy – to stir the potjie, chop the veggies, open that last can of beans, braai on. Check out the camping checklist on page 43 for more details.

6. Alcohol. Cold beers to cool you down on a hot summer's evening. Brandy to warm you up around the fire on a freezing night. Wine to make your food taste better. Just one thing though, whatever you do and no matter how desolate the road, don't drink and drive. Don't be stupid – it's really not worth it!

7. A Stash of Padkos. This always tastes better than the junk you buy next to the road. Pack in your favourite snacks to keep the hunger at bay. And support the locals – you'll find the best local produce along the way.

8. A Puncture Repair Kit. Or five. For those back roads that like to eat your car's tyres. If you're doing it right you'll have at least one puncture on your trip – if you're on the road for 70 days, that number tends to increase.

9. A Map. Yes, today many people diss the map for the GPS. Big mistake. Keep a map in your car (as detailed as you can find) – you'll need one when you least expect it. And if you're a guy you can keep your manhood and safely refuse to ask for directions.

10. Water. If you're taking the road less travelled, having a 5-litre container of water in every car is *always* a good idea.

11. A Decent Flask. One for coffee and one for water. Be nice to the planet – avoid buying *another* plastic bottle of water.

12. Sunglasses. A decent pair for driving – there's nothing worse than squinting into the sun – especially in rural areas. Chances are if you don't have visibility you can easily drive off a cliff, Thelma and Louise style. They made it look fun, but I'm guessing it's not. Sunglasses are also great for hiding telltale bloodshot eyes from the party you had the night before.

13. Toilet Paper and Wet Wipes. And a Spade. For when your girlfriend can no longer *knyp* and you have to pull over. Or when that dodgy (possibly horse-meat pie) you bought in a small town from the guy with only two front teeth *very suddenly feels like a very bad idea.* I'm not going to go into details. Just pack it.

14. Tents. For camping, obviously. But make sure everything is there *before* you hit the road. Missing a vital structure and some pegs is not fun when the wind is howling and it's pouring down.

15. First-aid Kit. You never know what might happen, so it's good to be prepared. We always suggest a couple of really-good-to-have-things: sunblock, aftersun, headache tablets, REHIDRAT®, charcoal tablets, band-aids and good old Dettol™.

16. A Hacky Sack. This is a good way to stretch your legs when you pull over to rest. Check the rules of playing hacky sack on page 87.

17. A Toolkit. Someone in your group needs to have a proper one in case of roadside or campsite emergencies.

18. Then some of my personal favourites to have in my car along the way: A little kit to keep **cuttings of plants** I see and like along the way – but be careful of doing this if you're crossing borders... smuggling is against the law, and try to avoid taking cuttings from forbidden areas... think Nature Reserves or people who will be really unhappy if you steal their plants; my **geologist pick** (I'm getting more interested in Africa); if your **camera** is your phone ignore this, otherwise take one to snap the many memories you're bound to make; and **biltong** (I made mine in the car while travelling – page 149).

19. Rechargeable Bluetooth Speaker Device. This means you can create your own party anywhere. Think of it as carrying a boom box on your shoulders... except better and louder.

Planning the Route...

Every journey has to start somewhere – usually with one single step, but before taking it my advice would be to start with a solid travel plan. As much fun as it is to embrace your inner Christopher Columbus, it's good to be prepared too. So plan your route... but be flexible and definitely find the road less travelled. Do research, check out what food they have locally, ask around, hear what people have to say, and know this: when too many people are talking about a certain place, chances are that it won't be as quiet as you want it to be...unless you actually want to go on a getaway similar to a Contiki tour.

When it came to planning our route for 70-odd crewmembers, we had no choice but to plan a logistical round route. And so, in a way it made sense that our journey started in Noordhoek, because that's where I live and it gave us all a couple of extra days to get our ducks in a row before hitting the road in earnest. One last note? When you're in bigger towns stock up on stuff you think you might not be able to find in the more desolate areas you're bound to travel to. It's not a great feeling when you really need something only to discover you can't get access to it for the next couple of weeks – so be travel ready!

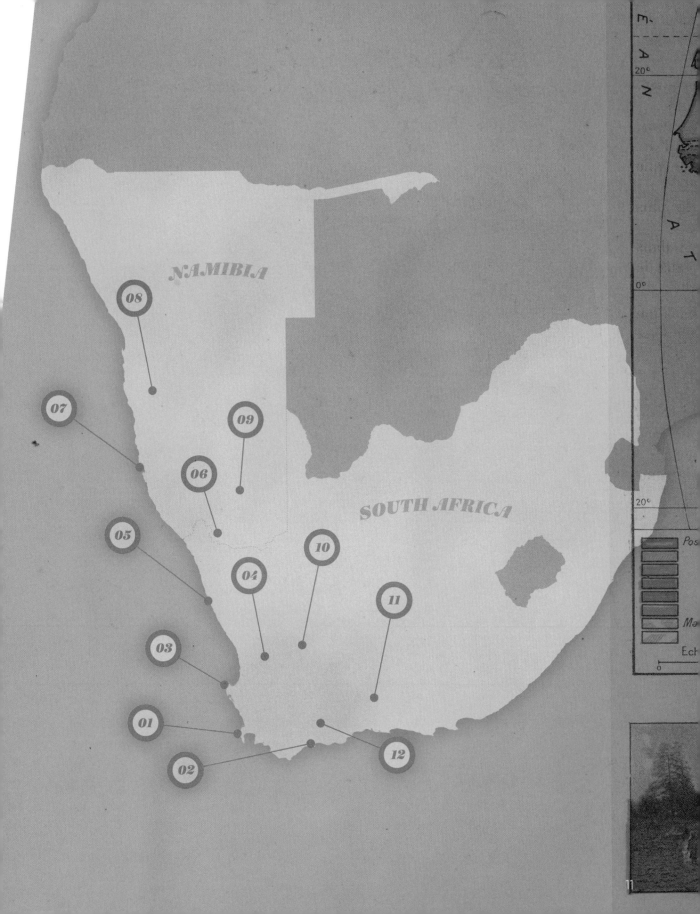

NAMIBIA

SOUTH AFRICA

08

07

09

06

05

04

03

10

11

01

02

12

11

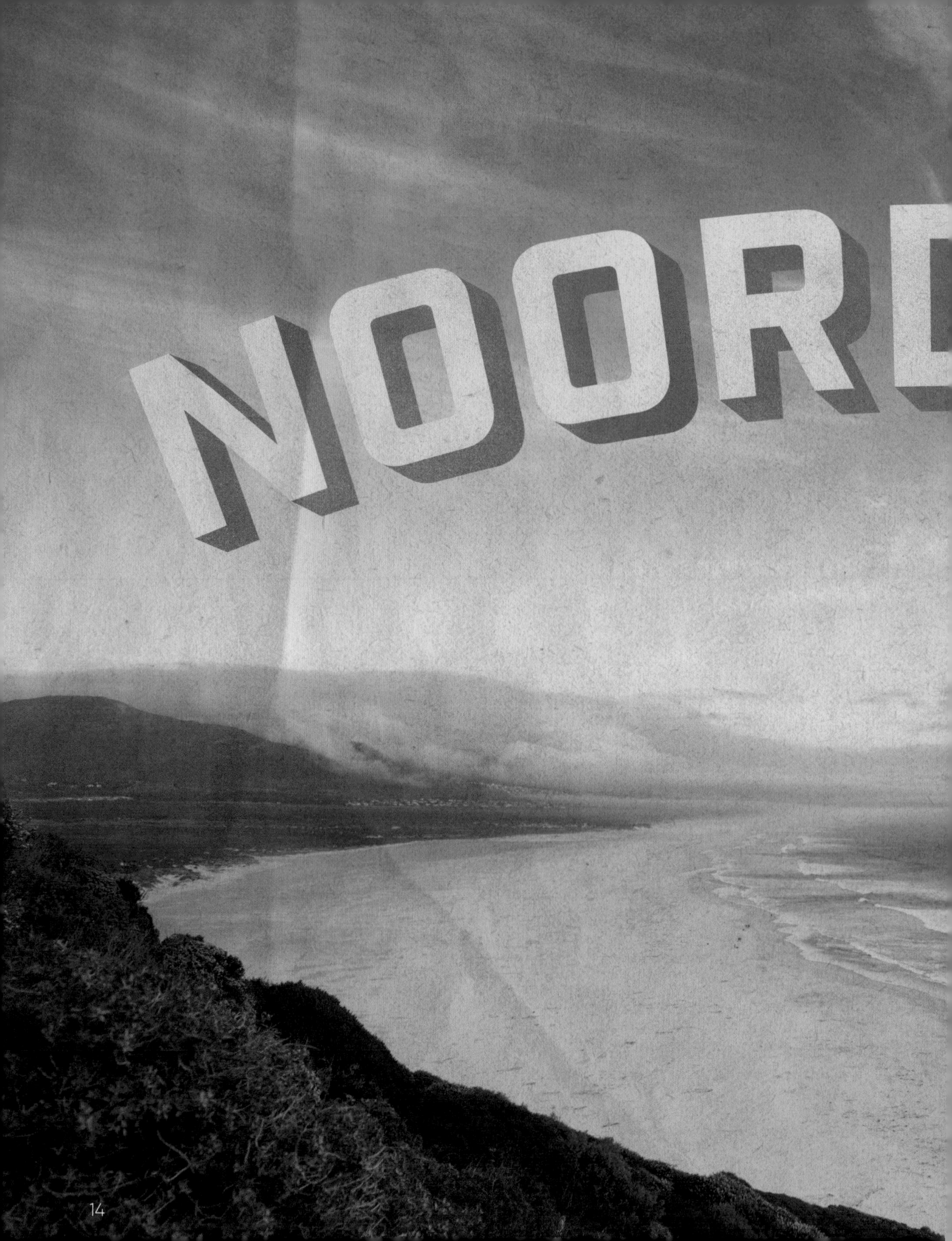
NOORD

DHOEK

Noordhoek happens to be my hood – and for a very good reason. It forms part of a protected area, which runs from the heart of the Table Mountain National Park in the Mother City right through to Cape Point in the south, where tourists think the Indian and Atlantic oceans collide. Noordhoek Valley remains one of Cape Town's best weekend destinations – for the pristine white, sandy beach that stretches for seven kilometres all the way to Kommetjie, for the infinite wetlands, the scattering of green coastal fynbos and for the area's rustic atmosphere. But one word of warning... beware the horsey people of Noordhoek (and surrounds). They're strange folk who tend to move in packs, and chances are if you don't speak 'horse' they won't understand a word that comes out of your mouth... and vice versa.

We kicked off our journey at Monkey Valley Resort in Noordhoek for what was going to be one of the most memorable road trips we'd ever been on – and trust me on this, we've been on plenty! The resort is situated at the foot of Chapman's Peak and chances are that if you've ever been a visitor to the Mother City, you've driven on this famous pass – unless it was closed due to rock-falls... she can get moody like that. It's from this vantage point that you'll notice the immensity and unspoilt beauty of South Africa's Atlantic coast – a feast for the eye for both locals and visitors alike.

the road trippers playlist

One of the most important things you'll ever have in your car when you're about to go on an adventure is music. It's one of those things that great memories are built around. This is some of the road tripping crew's favourite songs from their two-month trip. I think it's safe to say that you probably won't like all of the songs on the list, but there's never-spoken-about car etiquette that allows everyone at least one chance to play their favourite song – no matter how good or how bad. And if you don't like what they're playing, just grit your teeth and concentrate on the road. And if you do, open up the windows, stick your arm out and let it dance in the wind while you sing along.

1. **ENJOY THE SILENCE** (DEPECHE MODE)
2. **BEAUTY IN LITTLE THINGS** (BEBETTA *MIX)
3. **SWEET JANE** (COWBOY JUNKIES)
4. **STARGAZE** (XAVIER RUDD)
5. **BUT, HONESTLY** (FOO FIGHTERS)
6. **I'M ON FIRE** (BRUCE SPRINGSTEEN)
7. **ANIMAL** (MIIKE SNOW)
8. **PUNKROCKER** (TEDDYBEARS *FEAT. IGGY POP)
9. **CAPE COD KWASSA KWASSA** (VAMPIRE WEEKEND)
10. **US V THEM** (LCD SOUNDSYSTEM *LONDON SESSION)
11. **HOSANNA** (BOO!)
12. **FIREPROOF** (THE NATIONAL)
13. **GOOD LIFE** (ONEREPUBLIC)
14. **WHY'D YOU ONLY CALL ME WHEN YOU'RE HIGH?** (ARCTIC MONKEYS)
15. **TOO MUCH** (BONAPARTE)
16. **THIRSTY THURSDAYS MIX** (TOBY2SHOES)
17. **GIORGIO BY MORODER** (DAFT PUNK)
18. **SULTANS OF SWING** (DIRE STRAITS)
19. **DON'T SWALLOW THE CAP** (THE NATIONAL)
20. **ISLAND IN THE SUN** (WHEEZER)
21. **BABYLON** (DAVID GRAY)

22. **ALWAYS TAKE THE WEATHER WITH YOU** (CROWDED HOUSE)
23. **FLOAT ON** (MODEST MOUSE)
24. **NATURAL MYSTIC** (BOB MARLEY)
25. **NAMIBIA** (MIKE SMITH)
26. **SCIENCE KILLER** (THE BLACK ANGELS)
27. **ARIZONA** (KINGS OF LEON)
28. **SHE KEEPS THE HOME FIRES BURNING** (RONNIE MILSAP)
29. **DON'T STOP BELIEVIN'** (JOURNEY)
30. **I DROVE ALL NIGHT** (CELINE DION)
31. **PRIVATE DANCER** (TINA TURNER)
32. **SAIL** (AWOLNATION)
33. **PSYCHO KILLER** (TALKING HEADS)
34. **MANGO** (PAUL KALKBRENNER)
35. **SADNECCESARY** (MILKY CHANCE)
36. **EMMYLOU** (VANCE JOY)
37. **NO ONE KNOWS** (TEENAGE MUTANTS AND KANT)
38. **GHOST RIDERS IN THE SKY** (JOHNNY CASH)
39. **VOODOO CHILD** (JIMI HENDRIX)
40. **KEEP THE STREETS EMPTY FOR ME** (FEVER RAY)

Let's Talk About the Food...

The recipes in this book belong to many people from all walks of life. Some of them are mine. Some of them were inspired by the road. Some of them were made by the crew – after all, an army marches on its stomach! And then, as always, there were top chefs thrown into the mix. (This also meant that we got to tuck into some delicious fireside dishes along the way.) The first one is no stranger – Chef Bertus Basson. He has become part of the furniture and has been travelling with us since the very first season of *Ultimate Braai Master*. The second is Chef Petrus Madutlela, who joined us all the way from London and, after being homesick for many years, was happy to be back on familiar ground and embraced every kilometre of our journey. And, of course (in case you forgot), we were filming a reality braai series (we weren't just there for a good time!) and so it only seems right to share with you some of the best contestant recipes we got to taste.

The saying might be that too many cooks spoil the broth but, in this case and, when you get to share braai knowledge and ideas around a fire, too many cooks make for a great recipe collection.

A Fiery Start:
Fish & Prawn
CURRY

BY Syith & Preshen

To feed 12 friends, YOU NEED:

5 cardamom pods

2 cinnamon sticks

2 tablespoons of ground cumin

1 tablespoon of turmeric

1 tablespoon of ground coriander

½ cup of canola oil

4 onions, chopped

6 chillies, chopped

4 tablespoons of fish masala

4 tablespoons of masala spice mix

2 tablespoons of salt

1.5 kg tomatoes, grated

2 tablespoons of tomato paste

1 x 410 g tin of whole peeled tomatoes

2 tablespoons of tamarind paste

1 cup of water

2 heads garlic, sliced

1 kg prawns

2 kg smoked fish (choose your favourite, but make sure it's sustainable)

2 big handfuls of fresh coriander

Some things should be left to the experts. If you're looking to find a hipster sipping on an ethical double flat white, while donning skinny jeans, listening to Bon Iver tracks and using the words 'rad' and 'epic' as a description of everything that is rad and epic, go to Cape Town. If you want to learn how to drink copious amounts of *brandewyn en coke* without falling over, *langarm* and sing along to some one-man-band covering the greatest hits by Bob Dylan, Smokie and Creedence Clearwater Revival, then Pretoria is the place to be. If you want to eat the best Shisa Nyama, dance to music blaring out the boots of cars (and into the boots on your feet) and swig quarts of Castle Milk Stout, then go to Soweto. And if you're looking for a great surf, laid-back vibes and the 'so perfect it will make you sweat under your eyes and smack your lips together' curry, then Durban is where you should go. And if you can't go to Durban, then take Durban on the road with you... that's what we did.

Heat a large fireproof pan over hot coals and toast the cardamom, cinnamon, cumin, turmeric and ground coriander. When you do this, the moisture cooks off and the spices take on a warm and earthy flavour, which tastes totally different to raw spices. After about 5 minutes, add a glug of the canola oil then sauté the onions and chillies. Next add all the masala, salt and grated tomatoes and let it simmer for about 5 minutes before adding the tomato paste, tinned tomatoes, tamarind and water. Simmer for another 5 minutes, then add the garlic. After about 2 minutes, add the prawns and cook for 2 minutes before adding the fish. Cover the pan and simmer for 15 minutes. Add the fresh coriander just before tucking in. Serve with rice, sambals, roti and cold beer for the burn.

Make Your Own Quick Roti!

• •

This is a secret family recipe that Sherwyn (of Bushies Gone Wild) shared with me – he says it took him ages to perfect it, so count yourself lucky that you don't have to test, toss, swear and repeat for hours on end. Thanks for sharing this with us Sherwyn (or should we be thanking your mom or aunty?)!

• •

For 18–24 rotis,

YOU NEED:

3 cups of cake flour

a decent pinch of salt

3 tablespoons of butter, melted

1½ cups of rapidly boiling water

4 tablespoons of canola oil

• •

Mix the flour and salt together in a bowl, then make a well in the centre. Next, pour in the melted butter, hot water and oil and then mix it with a wooden spoon. Once properly combined, tip the dough out onto a clean surface and knead for a couple of minutes. Next, divide the dough and roll into balls. Sprinkle some flour onto the work surface and roll out each ball of dough. Heat a nonstick, fireproof pan over moderate coals, then cook the rotis, one at a time and on both sides, until golden and you see bubbles forming.

These rotis are best enjoyed with a proper curry.

WITSAND

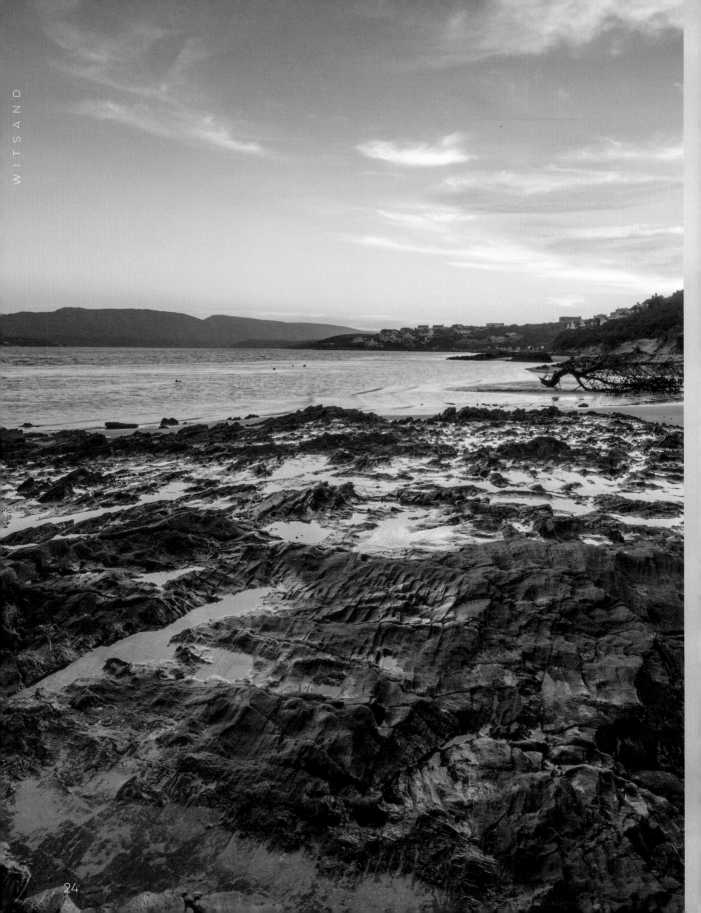

It's great to leave the noise of the city and head off into the big, wide open spaces of our country, but often you'll arrive at a place where there is nothing and anything you've forgotten is, well, forgotten, and then you have to make do with what you've got. Sometimes this is possible, but more often than not *that thing* you forgot to pack will be something important that you really can't do without. So try to plan the second stop of your road trip somewhere you can still pick up that toothbrush you left behind. You don't want to be the person who's stuck camping in the middle of nowhere and when bedtime comes realises you forgot your toothbrush and then have to use their partner's/best friend's/not-best-friend's dodgy looking one.

For this reason, we decided to head up to the east coast to a place close enough to get to some big towns so we could still organise all those forgotten things if we needed to. And so, after a week in Noordhoek, we finally hit the road in earnest, cars and trucks packed to the brim and lots of excitement in the air – especially for the 70 crewmembers who live and breathe for the open road and embrace a nomadic lifestyle whenever they can. About 280 kilometres later our convoy arrived in the picturesque town of Witsand, situated at the mouth of the Breede River. For those in the know, and for those who are not, this area is famous for being the playground of the Southern Right Whale – to the extent that it's been dubbed the whale nursery of southern Africa, although the folk in Hermanus might fight you tooth and nail on that – and this alone should see Witsand breaching the top of your travel bucket list at the right time of the year. But if the ocean's majestic gentle giants don't make your heart pump custard, then perhaps (and if you're an avid birdwatcher) the abundance of birdlife will. Still not convinced? Well, then maybe the following words will do the trick: Panoramic views. Brilliant boating. Best estuarine fishing in the country, especially for Kob, Grunter and Garrick. Yes, I knew I would convince some keen fishermen with that last bit. Hook, line and sinker.

After everyone had settled into their respective rooms at the Breede River Lodge (read: dropped their bags and found the bar), we had time to kill. And what you've got to understand about working on the road for two months straight, is that when we have downtime, it's a rare occasion, and we embrace it wholeheartedly. And so developed a raucous night of Breede River Lodge shooters and Beer Pong!

BEER PONG

Admittedly Beer Pong is an American pastime, so we were surprised that this was the main event at the local bar. But, as they say... when in Rome... or at the Breede River Lodge, do as the Breede River Lodgers do.

You know how there's always an underdog in life. The quiet, unsuspecting guy. The one you secretly root for in books, movies or sports. And beer pong. To everyone's surprise this particular underdog was Basil – the very sweet and innocent-looking, 60-something-year-old Pick n Pay truck driver. By the end of the night he had the bar cheering his name in unison as they watched every unsuspecting 20- to 30-year-old knock back beer after beer after being stupid enough to challenge him. So be warned. If you ever see this guy, don't challenge him... unless you're *really* thirsty.

1. Choose your partner.

2. Suss out your opponent. If it's anyone by the name of Basil, fake a wrist injury and walk away with your reputation intact.

3. Turn a table lengthways and place 10 cups at each end. Do this in the shape of a horizontal pyramid, with the point of the pyramid facing your opposition.

4. Pour equal amounts of beer into each cup.

5. Have a bucket of water handy – the ping-pong ball tends to hit some rather questionable surfaces throughout the game, so it's a good idea to rinse it before each shot. Unless you like the idea of getting hair (or worse things) in your teeth. (Although I've been told bacteria are good for your guts...)

6. Do a quick team huddle and end in the manly fist-bump and a shout-out of 'YEAH!' in deep, loud voices. If done right, this will intimidate the opposition.

7. Decide who goes first: Rock, paper, scissors – the winner gets the first shot.

8. Start the game: The idea is to get two balls per turn into your opponents' cups. You do this by aiming the ball at the cup and throwing it straight in – also called lobbing. Should it bounce before going in, your opponent (read: war enemy) now has the opportunity to swat it away.

9. Down-downs: By the end of each team's turn, count the cups with balls and drink accordingly. If the opposing team has two balls (one in each cup) then they have to down two beers, and so on. Once the beer has been drunk, the cups are removed from the table. Teammates take turns downing the beer, or if you're feeling kind, share the cup. If there are two cups to be drunk, then one goes to each player.

10. What if two balls land in the same cup? Well, that's worth three cups, with the third cup being downed by the person nominated by the attacking team.

11. The re-rack. Each team is allowed two re-racks per game. If called, the opposing team must rearrange their cups into a more condensed shape (as per the attacking team's instruction) – think triangles or diamonds. This makes it easier to land a shot.

12. Keep playing until one team has no more cups left.

For one quick game of beer pong, YOU NEED:

20 plastic draught cups

10 beers (if you're a girly-girl or a girly-guy (or really clever) get low-alcohol beers)

1 ping-pong ball

guts or naivety, or a combination of both

SOME GENERAL RULES:

1. Don't touch the ball before it bounces or before it goes into a cup. If you do, your opponent gets another shot/lob.

2. If the ball lands and balances on the cups' rims, don't try to blow the ball away. That's cheating.

3. Remove the ball before downing the beer. You don't want to lose the game because you choked and died. That's no fun for anyone.

4. On that note: Don't play this game and drive or operate heavy machinery. While games like these are fun, they're best enjoyed when you get to talk about it the next day.

Viskop SOP

BY *Piet & Frik*

For 3–4 bowls of soup,
YOU'LL NEED:

2 fennel bulbs, sliced

1 carrot, sliced

1 leek, sliced

1 onion, finely chopped

2 fish heads, cleaned

2 cups of KWV Sauvignon Blanc

2 cups of water

1 star anise

2 whole cloves

2 bay leaves

1 seeded chilli

salt and pepper to taste

One of my favourite things about being out in the great outdoors is to not only enjoy the space, but also nature's bounty and one of the best ways for me to do that is to go fishing. Nowadays we've become so disconnected from our food that when we actually get to catch a fish, you often think that the only usable part of it is the flesh. Well, you're wrong. All the bones can be used to make a stock, and the heads? Good old-fashioned *Viskop Sop* comes to mind. Way back when, making soup by cooking fish heads was borne out of necessity and will probably not appeal to many of you. But let me tell you, cooking this will make you think twice before throwing food into the bin. One of the challenges contestants faced on the road was to make their version of fish head soup, and I'm sorry to say that most of theirs tasted like fishy salty bathwater. Except for this one. In Bertus's words: 'I can eat a big bowl of this and be a very happy man.' And he's an award-winning chef, so it's got to be true, right? If you want to 'beef it up', add chunks of fish towards the end of the cooking time. Me? I like it just like this.

Put all the ingredients in a large potjie, put the lid on and simmer gently for 1 hour. Once done, remove all the whole spices and fish heads with a slotted spoon and serve the soup piping hot with crusty bread on the side. Some of the purists out there might want to push the soup through a muslin cloth first to get a nice clear soup, but it's up to you.

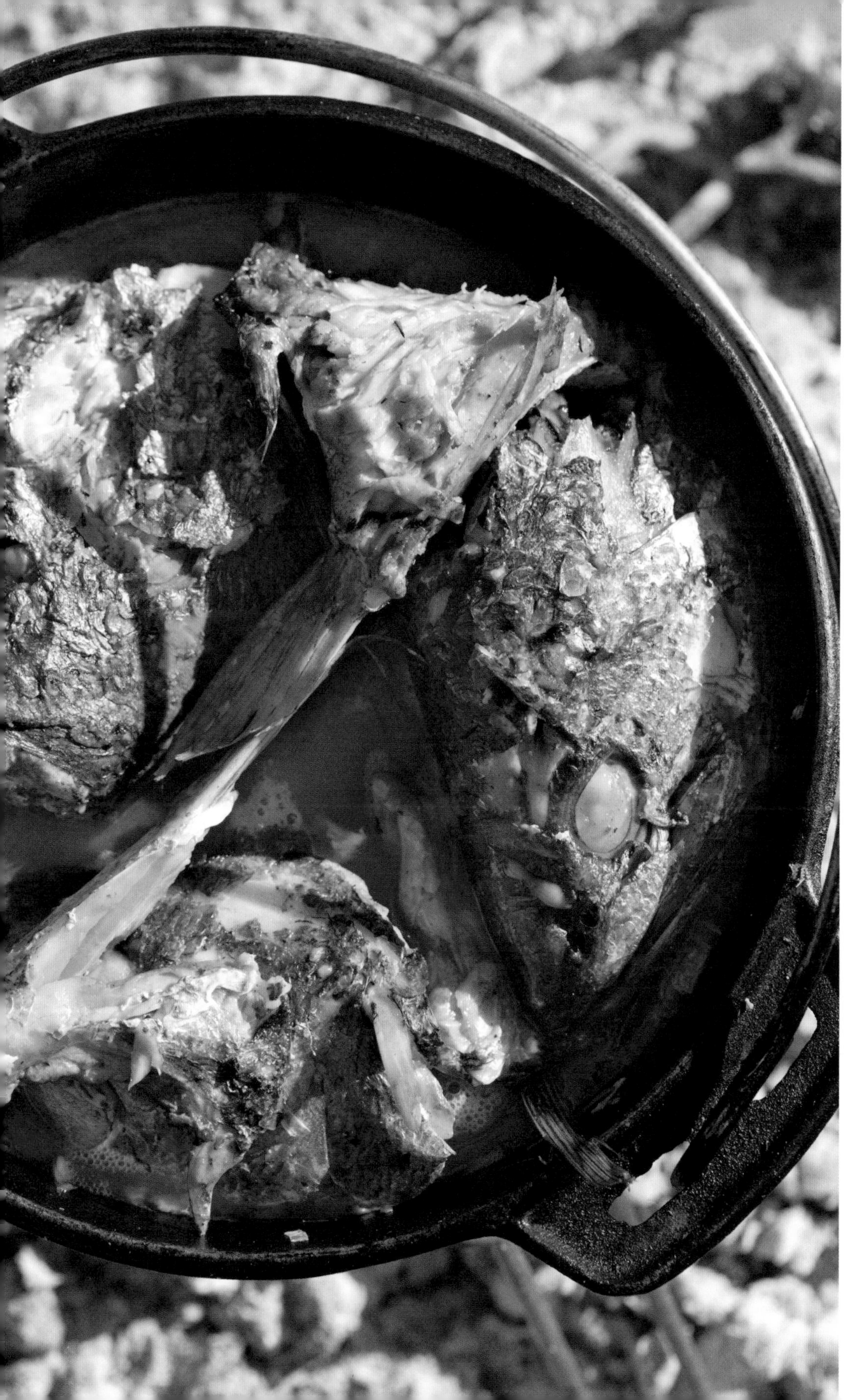

Braaied Brandy BANANA Splits

BY *Penny & Dee*

For 6 friends, YOU'LL NEED:

6 ripe bananas, unpeeled – one per friend

1 bottle of KWV Brandy (any year will do)

1 syringe (yes... a CLEAN one!)

100 g butter

2 tablespoons of brown sugar (or if you want it sweeter, add more)

a sprinkle of ground cinnamon

Injecting alcohol into fruit is the oldest trick in the book – especially popular with students who try to sneak alcohol into festivals and rugby matches. The most popular choice is definitely vodka and oranges. And they definitely never braaied it. So, make this if you happen to have some leftover padkos bananas lying in the back of your car and a bottle of brandy rolling around on the floor next to them.

Step 1: Inject each banana with brandy – as little or as much as you would like.

Step 2: Braai them over moderate coals, turning often and until the skin is dark brown all over.

Step 3: While the bananas are on the go, melt the butter in a small saucepan, then stir in the sugar until it's dissolved.

Step 4: Add a splash of brandy to the sauce and flambé, and then stir in the cinnamon.

Step 5: Remove the braaied bananas from the heat and, while they're still warm, slice them open, lengthwise.

Step 6: Drizzle brandy butter sauce over each banana and serve with ice cream, cream or custard.

Upside Down
BANANA

BY *Petrus Madutlela*

YOU'LL NEED:

250 g unsalted butter

1 cup of brown sugar

2 cinnamon sticks

4 star anise

*2 bunches of bananas,
peeled and sliced*

1 roll of short crust pastry

While we're on the topic of bananas... YUM! This is deliciously sweet and sticky – serve with dollops of real double-thick cream.

Melt the butter in a large, heavy-bottomed pan with a fireproof lid, then stir through the sugar until dissolved. Next, add the cinnamon and star anise and let it simmer for about 5 minutes over moderate coals – stirring continuously – then remove from the heat. Arrange the sliced bananas over the whole lot, then roll out the short crust pastry and lay it over the bananas. Tuck the overhanging dough around the sides, and prick the surface with a fork.

Pop the lid onto the pan, and scatter a few coals over the top. Bake over moderate coals for about 25 minutes or until golden on top. Remove the tart from the heat and allow to cool slightly, then place a wooden board over the top of the pan and carefully flip the pan over, so that the banana is on the top and the pastry at the bottom. Place it on the table with some bowls, double-thick cream and spoons and watch it get devoured faster than a heartbeat.

34

Bushie
DOUGHNUTS

BY *Sherwyn & Zane*

These beauties soon became a crowd favourite on the road – and who would have thought you can actually make something like doughnuts in the great outdoors and then pack them into your padkos stash for those endless drives where a sweet craving always hits and there's no shop in sight!

FOR THE DOUGHNUTS:

5 cups of cake flour

4 tablespoons of baking powder

1 tablespoon of bicarbonate of soda

½ cup of sugar

1 tablespoon of mixed spice

1 tablespoon of ground cinnamon

½ tablespoon of ground ginger

1 tablespoon of ground nutmeg

½ tablespoon of ground cloves

2 large free-range eggs

1½ cups of milk

100 g butter, melted

750 ml oil for frying

FOR DUSTING:

½ cup of sugar

4 tablespoons of ground cinnamon

To make the dough, put all the dry ingredients and spices into a large bowl. Whisk the eggs and milk together in a separate bowl, and then mix in the melted butter. Add the wet ingredients to the dry and combine thoroughly. If the dough is too sticky, simply rub a bit of oil over your hands and knead the dough until smooth. Make fist-sized balls then set aside. Heat the oil in a flat-bottom potjie over moderate coals and as soon as it's hot enough for frying (think French fries), gently drop the doughnuts into the hot oil. Deep-fry until golden and then use a slotted spoon to remove them from the oil. Put them on kitchen paper to drain.

Mix together the sugar and cinnamon and then dust the warm doughnuts generously. If you want to, you can dust them with plain icing sugar instead. Equally lekker and up to you!

Braised OCTOPUS Salad

FOR THE OCTOPUS:

a glug of olive oil

2 onions, chopped

2 carrots, chopped

1 stalk celery, chopped

1 leek, chopped

2 cloves garlic, crushed

a thumb of ginger, grated

3 bay leaves

4 star anise

1 octopus, cleaned

350 ml soy sauce

FOR THE SALAD:

1 big handful of your favourite lettuce leaves

a very small handful of pickled ginger

1 ripe avocado, peeled and sliced

1 handful of walnuts

FOR THE DRESSING:

30 ml soy sauce

⅓ cup of peach chutney

a big glug of olive oil

The first thing you need to know when cooking octopus is how to tenderise it, because this highly intelligent sea monster will be as tough as old rubbery boots if you don't. So how do you do this? Well there are many myths and many theories that still sit on the fence. One I've learnt over the years is to cook the octopus with a wine cork in a mirepoix (chopped onions, celery and carrots), on a hard boil for 1 hour. The cork is supposed to cause a chemical reaction, which softens the octopus. Other thoughts on tenderising include brining, marinating, massaging, and banging the living daylights out of it. It's no wonder that no one really makes octopus at home – the mere thought of just the preparation of getting it tender is daunting. But there are simpler ways of doing it, like in this recipe from Yusuf and Stephen.

Heat a medium-sized potjie over moderate coals, then add a glug of olive oil. Sauté the onions, carrots, celery, leek, garlic, ginger, bay leaves and star anise for about 10 minutes until fragrant. Add the octopus and fry until caramelised, then pour in the soy sauce and 2 litres of water and simmer until tender (this should take about 1½ hours). The moment the octopus is tender, remove the potjie from the heat. Take the octopus out and cut it into bite-sized chunks, then toss with the lettuce and ginger. Mix all the dressing ingredients together and drizzle over the salad. Garnish with slices of ripe avocado and a sprinkle of walnuts.

BY Yusuf & Stephen

37

PATER

After an adventurous (and perhaps a little too raucous) stay at the Breede River Lodge, it was time to pack up everything again and change direction from east to west and so we drove to the fishing hamlet of Paternoster, about 380 kilometres from Witsand. Every road trip should have what I call the 'ebb and flow'. Like many of the small seaside towns scattered up and down the West Coast, Paternoster boasts some of the best seafood you'll ever get your hands on – especially if you arrive in time for crayfish season. The charm of Paternoster lies in two things: the first is the white-washed beach houses scattered all along the coast, and the second is that it's one of the last remaining traditional fishing villages on the West Coast. When you meet some of the locals, you'll be well impressed with the rich fishing history and their unrivalled knowledge of the ocean's bounty. As a fun fact, I could add that this is also home to South Africa's very first 'Redro' fish paste factory – I'm sure anyone over the age of 30 will appreciate this.

If seafood and fish paste aren't your cup of tea then perhaps the West Coast's spectacular wild flower season from July to October will be. Unfortunately for us, we were there about a month too early so didn't get to stop and smell the wild flowers, but what we lacked in flower power we more than made up for in the brilliant fish braais we enjoyed at the water's edge.

Extreme CAMPING

Just outside of Paternoster is the Cape Columbine Nature Reserve and inside this reserve you'll spot the towering red-and-white lighthouse on Castle Rock – the last manually controlled lighthouse in South Africa, which dates back to 1936. And if you happen to be on a boat you should easily spot it from about 50 kilometres offshore.

It was time for contestants to experience one of the best camping spots in our country (at least, I think it is) in Tietiesbaai. While some of the women looked less than pleased with what would be their accommodation for the next couple of days, it was soon forgotten once they started drinking in the incredible views of the rough and unforgiving West Coast seas. While you might think that we were cruel to send them into their tents on the coast in the middle of winter, that's not really the case. The West Coast is generally rain free, and while the rest of the Cape is merciless and stormy during winter, you'll usually find good weather here during the country's coldest season. Admittedly the first night was a little windy, but we made sure they were prepared to camp like pros and able to fend for themselves and eat like kings and, after all, there's nothing a few drinks and the warmth of the African TV can't fix when you're feeling miserable, right? If you're going on a road trip, you're always planning for something, so go for the crayfish festival, or the wild flowers – and if you're not travelling the West Coast for anything other than to get out of town, plan your route around the weather.

Should you ever decide to go camping (in the middle of winter), here are some basic things you should have with you to weather the storm. It's a basic list, so feel free to add to it – camping runs in our blood and we're all pretty good at it.

● ●

1. A decent sleeping bag. If you don't have one, make sure you have a decent girlfriend or boyfriend to keep you warm.

2. A roll-up mattress – the days of sleeping straight on the ground are over, for me at least.

3. Proper hiking shoes. This is the whole point of being in the great outdoors – exploring. You definitely don't want to be stuck in the campsite for your entire stay.

4. Flashlights and solar jars. Very handy if you don't feel like stumbling around in the dark and the solar light jars are great for dinner time or to put in your tent.

5. Clothes that will protect you from the worst elements – like rain, wind, sun and freezing cold. You never know what nature will throw at you.

6. Fold-up chairs and a table or two. It just makes life easier and more comfortable.

7. A proper cooler box (like a Colemans – they last for years and years) to keep all your fresh stuff fresh.

8. A tent (obviously) and all the pegs and things you need to secure it to the ground.

9. Games and other stuff to keep you entertained (check out pages 87-89 for ideas).

10. Loads of firewood to make fires for those epic braais you'll be having and staring into late into the night. Don't make the mistake of expecting to find firewood locally – that's not always the case.

11. Something to drink – always. On that note, pack a decent flask. And a big jerry can of water.

12. All the cooking and braaiing utensils you can think of, including a braai grid and braai tongs.

13. Coffee and rusks. It's the easiest breakfast to have when all you feel like is getting up and exploring without the hassle of cooking up a feast.

Whole BRAAIED FISH
With Rustic Pesto, Tapenade & Ash Tomatoes

FOR THE TAPENADE:

about 2½ cups of good-quality calamata olives, pitted

2 anchovies, chopped

1 small clove garlic, chopped

1 decent glug of olive oil

juice of ½ lemon

2 teaspoons of capers

Very finely chop and mix together all the tapenade ingredients.

FOR THE RUSTIC PESTO:

a handful of pine nuts, toasted

olive oil – just enough to make a paste

2 cloves garlic

a couple of big handfuls of fresh basil

1 handful of grated Parmesan cheese

a decent squeeze of lemon juice

salt and pepper to taste

FOR SERVING:

vine tomatoes

toasted pine nuts

olive oil

salted pepper to taste

lemon wedges

BY *Bertus Basson*

This is the complete opposite of Gareth's Vis (page 51). It takes a little bit more effort, but it's well worth it if you've got the time. Which Bertus did.

Prepare the Fish: Bertus used a Sea Bream and left the head on. You can leave the head on. That's entirely up to you. But please gut the fish, and clean it properly. And the second important thing? Do it outside... it gets messy. My advice is to do it over some newspaper laid out on a table so that it's easy to clean later.

Start this by holding the fish securely, then scraping the scales off the fish using a butter knife. Do this from the tail towards the head, in quick movements. Run down to the ocean and rinse the fish in the seawater, then run back up to your makeshift prep table. Using a sharp knife, cut into the belly, from the tail up to the head, then remove the entrails with your hands. Then run back down to the ocean and give the fish another proper rinse (watch out for any seagulls lurking above your head... they're fast). Once done, pat dry and move the fish onto a clean surface.

Score the skin of the fish, on both sides, then rub generously with salt on the outside as well as inside the belly. Leave it for about 30 minutes (just enough time for you to start your fire and make the pesto and tapenade), then wipe off the salt.

For the Rustic Pesto: Put the nuts, olive oil and garlic in a mortar and pestle and bash it together until you have a paste. Add the basil leaves, a few at a time, and keep on bashing and grinding. When you have a smooth(ish) green paste, add the Parmesan and the lemon juice and bash it one last time. Season to taste. Done!

Braai: Put the fish inside a sandwich grid then braai over moderate coals for about 20 minutes, turning often – whatever you do, don't overcook the fish!

While the fish is on the braai, take a couple of tomatoes (on the vine) and pop them straight onto warm ashes and roast them until the skin is blistered.

Plate: This is the pretty part. Take a large wooden cutting board and place the whole braaied fish in the centre, top with the tapenade, the basil pesto and a scattering of toasted pine nuts. Drizzle with olive oil, season with salt and pepper, and serve lemon wedges on the side.

Have this on a special occasion, with great friends, whatever sides you feel like serving and ice-cold KWV Sauvignon Blanc.

THE PANTY BAR

Yes. You read that right. It's a bar and it's filled with... panties. A canopy of them hovering above your head while you *kuier* with your friends. I suspect this must be Ronnie's Sex Shop's dirtier, raunchier cousin (the one that the family always gossip about over tea and scones).

It's quite a beautiful sight to see for any hot-blooded man. Okay, it's also a little weird. You know the saying 'don't air your dirty laundry in public? Well here it's highly recommended – but only panties – they're not interested in men's underwear. Legend has it this bar used to be a jail before it became the final resting place for many unsuspecting, tipsy, daring women's underwear.

There's not a whole lot more to say about the panty bar, other than that it's a typical, unpretentious small-town watering hole, which usually guarantees hours of fun. So pop in and leave your dirty *broeks* behind, if you dare...

U-turn SARDINES

BY *Bertus Basson*

FOR THE SARDINES:

12 fresh sardines, gutted

metal skewers

1 potato, roughly cut into 12 cubes

FOR THE BASTING SAUCE:

a couple of chillies, seeded and chopped (how many you use is up to how hot you like them)

3 cloves garlic, crushed and chopped

about 1 cup of tomato sauce

juice of 2 lemons

about 2 tablespoons of coriander seeds, toasted and crushed

salt and pepper to taste

a couple of pinches of brown sugar

> **Skewered sardines, braaied over moderate coals, Portuguese style. Serve with fresh bread.**

Bertus made these while we were at the Beach Camp. Not many people are fans of the humble sardine, but try making them the Bertus way and you might just change your mind. In fact, I'm pretty sure you will.

Sardines are small enough to actually not have to gut, but they do need to be cleaned. Hold them under running water (or in seawater if that's nearby) and rub the scales off with a butter knife (or just use your thumbnail). Once you've cleaned all the sardines, set them aside.

Put all the basting sauce ingredients into a fireproof saucepan over moderate coals and stir the sauce until the sugar has dissolved, then set it aside.

Next, take the sardines and the skewers. Stick the sharp end of the skewer just above the tail part of the sardine – straight through, then gently into the fleshy part just below the head. What you want is a sardine that is now in the shape of a U. Take one cube of raw potato and stick the skewer into it – this will prevent the sardine from slipping out. Once you've skewered all 12 sardines, carefully put them on top of a braai grid, and start basting them in the spicy tomato sauce. Keep turning and basting as you go, until they're cooked through – this shouldn't take more than 5 minutes. Serve on a platter, drizzled with leftover basting sauce, a squeeze of lemon and fresh bread to dunk into all those lekker juices.

Visserman VIS

BY Gareth Beaumont

Real fishermen will tell you not to over-complicate fish – that the flavour should speak for itself – especially if you just caught it and it's so fresh that it blinked two seconds ago. And my friend Gareth Beaumont is one of those (no, not a fish that blinked two seconds ago... he's a fisherman). Here's his recipe for the ONLY way to braai a fish when you've just caught one. Simple and delicious.

. . . .

ALL YOU NEED IS:

olive oil

paprika

black pepper

fresh Sea Bream/whatever fish you've caught (ok... or bought at your local fishmonger – just make sure that it's a sustainable choice)

HOW TO BUTTERFLY FISH:

When you butterfly a fish you're doing two things: you're creating a bigger surface for flavour, and you can now fit the fish into a sandwich grid to braai it quickly and more evenly.

To butterfly a fish, you need a sharp knife, a cutting board and a pair of scissors. And a cleaned (scaled and gutted) whole fish.

1. Using sharp scissors, cut the fish open along the backbone, from head to tail.

2. Next, cut off the head – but keep it for Viskop Sop (page 28) or stock.

3. Make an incision down the centre of each fillet, but be careful not to cut through the skin.

4. Fold the fish open – back-side down, flesh-side up.

5. Remove any small bones from the meat – check with your fingers to find these and pick them out with pliers or tweezers.

Rub olive oil onto the flesh-side of your butterflied fish, followed by the paprika and black pepper. Braai over moderate coals for 5–10 minutes a side. Gareth says the fish is perfectly cooked when you pop a matchstick into the flesh and it falls straight through. Season to taste and serve with lemon.

BY *Justin Bonello*
Classic
MUSSELS

YOU'LL NEED:

about 1 kg fresh mussels

1 cup of white wine

1 handful of fresh parsley, chopped

a couple of big knobs of butter

4 cloves garlic, crushed and chopped

juice of 2 lemons

cracked black pepper to taste

a couple of chillies, seeded and chopped

When it comes to the full flavours of fresh West Coast food, my favourite remains the black mussel. I'm a firm believer that you shouldn't mess around with the natural taste of fresh seafood too much. I've been making these simple mussels for years, and it never fails to impress or taste delicious.

HOW TO CLEAN MUSSELS:

If you harvest your own mussels and want to get rid of all the sand and grit, soak them in fresh seawater for a couple of hours and they'll spit out the sand. No one likes to end up with a gritty mouthful of sand, but if you've got no choice just go for it. If you're going to serve the mussels in the shell, it's also a good idea to scrub them clean. And remember to pull out the beards after steaming them open – they might be all the rage in men's fashion these days... not so true with mussels.

Once you've cleaned the mussels, pop them into a potjie, add the white wine and fresh parsley, put the lid on and place onto the coals. Let the mussels steam until they pop open, then take them off the heat immediately. Spoon all the mussels into a separate bowl and don't get rid of any of that juice in the pot. Check through the mussels and toss out any ones that didn't open up – unless you're planning seafood poisoning for dessert (chances are that if they didn't open, then they're dead). Remove the mussels from their shells (toss the shells back into the sea) and when you're 100% sure you won't kill any of your nearest and dearest, it's time to add the three things that are going to make these mussels out of this world: butter, garlic and lemon, and I like to do three variations. So choose one then do the following:

1. Melt the butter in a potjie, add the garlic, a little bit of that reserved water and the mussels and heat through. Serve.

2. Melt the butter in a potjie, add lemon, a splash of the reserved water and black pepper, then the mussels. Heat through and serve.

3. Melt the butter, add a splash of reserved water and chopped chillies (as much or as little as you like), stir though the mussels and serve.

Serve your favourite kind of mussels, straight out of the pot while still piping hot, to your pack of hungry wolf friends, with loads of fresh bread to wipe up all that lekker butter sauce.

Mussels IN CURRY Cider

900 g fresh mussels, cleaned and beards removed

1 fennel bulb, sliced (keep the fronds and stalks)

a knob of butter

1 large onion, finely chopped

2 cloves garlic, finely chopped

2 teaspoons of curry paste

1 cup of apple cider (and one extra for you to sip on)

300 ml fresh cream

salt and pepper

a small bunch of fresh coriander

crusty bread for serving

You should know one thing about Yvonne Short, and one thing only. She is one of the most incredible cooks that I've ever met and she has a world of experience in all things culinary. Make these beauties and tell me I'm wrong. Exactly.

Once you've cleaned all the dirt and grit off the mussels, set them aside. Bring about 2 cups of water to a simmer in a potjie, then add the fennel fronds and mussels. Steam the mussels for 3–4 minutes, until the shells are just open, then take them out (make sure to throw away any unopened mussels). Keep about ½ cup of the liquid from the pot. In a separate potjie, melt the butter then fry the chopped onion, garlic and sliced fennel. Once the onions are nice and soft, stir through the curry paste and the ½ cup of mussel water, the cider and the cream. Have a taste and season with salt and pepper, then take the mussels off the heat. Sprinkle fresh coriander over the top, and serve with crusty bread and good wine!

AGENT FOR
PREEDY'S WELL KNOWN
SHELL
X-100
MOTOR OI
ost-Str.

DUSTER
CZ 43 JG GP

REG. T. M. 57

CEDER

After spending the first couple of weeks living and breathing a coastal lifestyle, it was time for the beachbum-crew to hit the road once again, and so the convoy slowly made its way inland, snaking its way through the dramatically changing and beautifully painted landscapes of the Cederberg. Situated roughly 200 kilometres from Paternoster (depending on the route you take), this protected area envelops about 182 000 hectares of Cape fynbos and has the most incredible rock formations in the Western Cape. There are over 2 500 rock-sites – many of them are easily accessible if you're willing to hike, so make sure you take a decent pair of hiking boots with you. Another highlight of this area is that it's the Rooibos capital of the country, which of course gave us an opportunity to make some deliciously boozy spiced tea. But I get ahead of myself.

RBERG

With so many things to do in the Cederberg even the most hardcore adventurer will be spoilt for choice. My only advice? Do it slowly. That's how you discover the hidden treasures of a place (those secret places locals like to keep to themselves) – when you slow down the pace, I promise you'll have the most memorable moments with your friends. One last thing I'll say about the Cederberg (before I start to sound like a travel brochure) is this: the landscape does wonders for your soul and it's the kind of place where you'll find yourself breathing in deeply and smiling, realising just how lucky we are to live in this country.

LAKE
Swimming

OK, it was a dam, but the word 'lake' just sounds so much more impressive.

The thing that keeps this agricultural heartland alive in the harsh, unforgiving summer months is the Bulshoek Dam, which carves its way for about 10 kilometres through the lush green farmlands. And we were lucky enough to have a part of this dam all to ourselves.

It was another day off for the crew – and as you know by now (if you've been reading this book) is that these are as rare as hens' teeth. We were staying at the Rondeberg Resort (just off the N7)

and instead of the usual raucous behaviour the crew opted to chill out next to the dam, to fish, to make some lekker food, and to laze around on blankets, reading, playing board games, listening to music and sipping on cold beers. It almost felt like summer and it was the perfect excuse to dive off the jetty and into the icy cold water for those who needed to remind themselves that they are, in fact, still alive. This is the way the outdoors should be embraced: by just enjoying what nature offers to us freely – something we often take for granted when we get lost in the hustle and bustle of our city lifestyles.

Faber's BAIT

YOU NEED:

2 cups of water

2 cups of maize meal

1 cup of cake flour

Andrew Faber is the Assistant Director on the show, but more than that he is an avid fisherman. Wherever we went, if there was a small chance that there might be fish in the body of water, *that's* where you'd find him. And usually a crowd of guys around him, drinking brandy and pretending to fish. And this has to be said about Faber: he's actually a good fisherman. Not sure if it's the combination of patience and skill or if the magic recipe is his bait, but more often than not he gets the fish. Below is his formula for bait, which he uses when fishing in fresh water. Give it a bash – you never know what you might catch!

Pour the water into a potjie and bring it to the boil, then stir in the maize meal and the flour. Keep stirring until properly combined and sticky – about 5 minutes should do the trick. Next, get ready to burn your hands. Tip the bait out onto a surface and start kneading. Do this for at least 5 minutes until pliable. Go to your cooler box and dunk your scorched hands into the ice. Divide the bait into three equal-sized balls then add the flavours. Faber's favourites are **honey**, **curry powder** and **vanilla essence** – but not combined! Take one ball, make a dent in it and squirt in 2–3 tablespoons of honey. Close it up and knead it a bit more to combine. If you choose vanilla, add about 2 teaspoons to another ball in the same way you did the honey, and if curry powder is what you're after, then add 2 tablespoons of that. Anyone who's ever fished will know how much bait to use but for the newbies out there, tear off a chunk roughly the size of your thumb, then secure it around the hook in the shape of a kite or pyramid. Play around with the three different types of bait – see what works. There are no solid rules here, except for one: always have cold beer (in summer) or good whiskey (in winter) close by. Now go fishing.

This one has been a winner with my family and friends for years, so it seems only right that I share it with you. The best thing about this potjie and the secret to why it tastes different to normal lamb potjies is because you braai the lamb before layering it into the potjie. That way you get that lovely smoky flavour that you can only get from the fire.

Braaied Lamb & Tomato
POTJIE
with Gnocchi

BY Justin Bonello

FOR THE POTJIE:

2–3 kg free-range Karoo lamb knuckles

seasoned flour for dusting

a glug of oil

1 onion, chopped

3–4 cloves garlic, crushed

2–3 leeks, sliced

2 x 400 g tins good-quality baby tomatoes or whole tomatoes

300–500 ml organic beef stock (this gives the basic flavour to your potjie, so only the best will do)

about 1 cup of KWV Merlot

1 small handful of sweet basil – both dried and fresh

1 small handful of dried oregano

salt and pepper to taste

First up, and to get that lekker smoky braai flavour, seal the lamb on all sides on a braai grid over hot coals then, once it's cooled down slightly, toss it in seasoned flour. Heat up a potjie, then caramelise the seasoned lamb in batches and set aside. Add a glug of oil to the potjie then fry the onion, garlic and leeks until soft and fragrant, then return the caramelised lamb. Scrape some coals to the side to reduce the heat and, while the lamb is gently simmering, add the tins of tomatoes, beef stock and red wine. Stir in the dried herbs, season to taste and let your potjie slowly whisper for a couple of hours until the meat just about falls off the bone. While the potjie is simmering away, make the potato gnocchi (or if you made it the night before, even better!).

CEDERBERG

ORANGE
WRAPPERS
BEAN &
SONS
SALE
WRAPPERS
TOMATO

FOR THE GNOCCHI:

1 kg potatoes

300 g cake flour

3 free-range egg yolks

1 teaspoon of salt

TO SERVE:

*1 punnet of fresh vine-ripened
cherry tomatoes (still on
the vine)*

*1 generous handful of shaved
pecorino or Parmesan cheese*

fresh parsley & basil, chopped

Wrap each potato in tinfoil and then bake them in moderate coals until soft (about 30 minutes). Keep turning them to prevent them from burning. Next, and while they're still hot, cut the potatoes in half and scoop the insides into a mixing bowl; mash until smooth. Stir the flour into the hot mashed potatoes, little bits at a time. (It is essential that the potatoes are still hot, because the heat activates the gluten in the flour.) Add the egg yolks and the salt. Hold your hand in the shape of a stiff, motionless claw (think Edward Scissor hands style) and mix the flour by taking that claw and jabbing (yes, really) it into the mashed potato and eggs. What you're looking for is a workable, pliable dough that almost sticks to your fingers. When the eggs and potatoes are properly combined, roll the dough into sausage-like shapes (about 3 cm in diameter) and double wrap in clingfilm, making sure it's completely airtight. And yes, should you need to do this, now is a good time to go stick your scorched hand in an ice bucket.

About 40 minutes before your potjie is going to be ready, simmer the 'sausages' in water for 15–20 minutes with the clingfilm on. Put the fresh vine tomatoes over moderate coals until blistered. While the tomatoes are over the coals, shock the gnocchi in ice-cold water to stop the cooking process, then remove the wrapping and slice it into bite-sized chunks. Arrange them on top of the potjie, making sure you submerge the pieces so they will soak up some of those lovely juices. Add the blistered fresh tomatoes to the potjie, simmer for 20 minutes more, then remove from the heat.

Serve with a generous handful of shaved parmesan and chopped fresh parsley and basil.

POTATO SKINS:

If you have any energy left, take the potato skins you had leftover from making the gnocchi and deep-fry until crispy. Drain on kitchen paper, season with coarse salt and serve with your favourite dip as a snack.

Mom's Chicken
POTJIE

BY *Petrus Madutlela*

If you watched the third season of *Ultimate Braai Master*, you'll know two things about chef Petrus: one, he has the most dazzling smile – blinding at times, and two, he loves his mother's chicken potjie recipe. It's a nostalgic taste that reminds him of his childhood, and sometimes that's all you need in a plate of food. Even though this is the simplest of recipes, and not something that would be defined as chef food, it's a taste of home for Petrus – a humble but delicious food memory that has a firm place in his heart.

YOU NEED:

a glug of canola oil

1 whole free-range chicken, cut into 8 portions

2 carrots, chopped

2 onions, chopped

500 g potatoes, peeled and quartered

about 2 cups of water

salt and black pepper to taste

Heat a potjie over moderate coals, then add a glug of canola oil and fry the chicken portions until golden brown. Next, add the carrots and onions and fry for another 5 minutes, or until the onions are fragrant and soft. Layer in the quartered potatoes, add the water, season with salt and black pepper and cover with the potjie lid. Scrape away some of the coals to reduce the heat and slowly simmer the potjie for 1–1½ hours. Serve with your favourite kind of pap (page 183).

Vegetarian POTJIE

BY *Bertus Basson*

Making vegetarian food can be super boring, but making a fun pot can liven things up a little... especially if you serve it with a big chunk of the butternut bread. This isn't a real recipe... just some guidelines and suggestions from Bertus for you to play around with when you've got to make a vegetarian potjie.

One.

Parboil some potatoes. Then sauté them in loads of butter, add some sliced onion, crushed garlic and fresh parsley. The potatoes are done when golden.

Two.

Slice some eggplants (brinjals). Toss the slices in olive oil, salt and pepper, then grill over the fire on both sides.

Three.

Make a kick-ass tomato sauce. (Or if you're a lazy cook, mix together 1 tin of chakalaka and 1 tin of tomato and onion smoor.)

Four.

Start the layers. Put the golden sautéed spuds in the bottom of a flat-bottom potjie. Layer the grilled eggplant over the potatoes. Scoop whichever tomato concoction you came up with over the eggplant.

Five.

Play around. Feel free to add some sautéed spinach or fresh basil. Or any of your favourite veggies and fresh herbs.

Six.

Make it super cheesy. Sprinkle generous amounts of grated Parmesan over the whole lot. Heck, follow this with crumbled feta.

Seven.

Bake it. Over moderate coals. Lid on. Coals on the top. Until golden brown.

Eight.

Tuck in. Have a giant chunk of butternut bread on the side. Sharing with meat-eating friends is optional.

SAFETY MATCHES

Butternut BREAD

BY *Bertus Basson*

For 3 loaves of delicious bread,
YOU NEED:

1 kg white bread flour

700 ml water

1 x 10 g packet dried yeast

40 g sugar

40 g salt

1 butternut, peeled and cut into small chunks

olive oil for drizzling

salt and pepper

1 small handful of maize meal for dusting

1 handful of pumpkin seeds

Make the dough by mixing together the flour, water, yeast, sugar and salt. Put the dough on a clean, floured surface and start kneading it. Initially the dough will feel quite soft, but keep kneading it until it's smooth and elastic. This is going to take some time and a bit of strength, but keep going – it's well worth it. Once done, put the dough in a large bowl, cover it with a dishtowel and pop in a warm spot to prove. While the dough is doubling in size, get on with the butternut.

Put the cubed butternut in a tray, drizzle with olive oil and season to taste, then cover with tinfoil. Place it over moderate coals and slowly roast it until cooked and caramelised.

When the dough has doubled in size, knock it down, and then butter-grease three flat-bottom potjies and dust them out with maize meal. Divide the dough into three equal portions and place in the three greased potjies. Arrange the butternut chunks on top, sprinkle over the pumpkin seeds and then set the pots aside to let the dough rise by one-third its size. Now it's time to finally place the potjie lids on top and to bake the bread over low coals, with a few coals scattered over the top of each lid to create an oven effect. There is no exact baking time, but be careful of too much heat – it burns easily, so check every now and then. The bread is ready when it's golden on top and when you stick a skewer inside it should come out clean and not doughy.

Once baked to perfection, turn the bread out and have a slice immediately, with lashings of real farm butter. Enjoy on its own or with your favourite *potjiekos* or *braaivleis*.

FOR THE OXTAIL:

2 kg oxtail

1 x 200 ml bottle of concentrated liquid beef stock

2 cups of cake flour

2 tablespoons of ground ginger

2 tablespoons of ground coriander

3 tablespoons of coriander seeds

2 tablespoons of fennel seeds

2 star anise

5 rashers of streaky bacon, chopped

1 cup of olive oil

2 large leeks, sliced

4 stalks celery, sliced

4 large carrots, chopped

1 chunk of fresh ginger, julienned

4 large cloves garlic, chopped

2 cups of chicken stock

3 tablespoons of green peppercorns (in brine)

4 fennel bulbs, whole

2 cups of dry white wine

pepper to taste

4 large, semi-ripe pears, peeled and left whole

STILTON GNOCCHI:

4 large potatoes

1½ cups of cake flour

6 free-range egg yolks

1 cup of crumbled Stilton or blue cheese

salt to taste

Fennel & Pear
OXTAIL
with Stilton Gnocchi

BY Lesley & Rod

Pear and blue cheese is a classic combination. At first we thought it would be a bit odd in a potjie with oxtail, but the results were incredible. This is Lesley's recipe and she's perfected it over the years.

Coat the meat in the beef stock (undiluted) and sear on a braai grid over moderate to hot coals. Mix together the flour, ground ginger and ground coriander and use this to dust the oxtail (once cooled). Next, grab two pans and dry toast the whole coriander seeds, fennel seeds and star anise in one pan and sauté the bacon in the other pan.

Heat the olive oil in a potjie over moderate to hot coals, then sauté the leeks, celery, carrots, ginger and garlic. Once softened, remove from the potjie and set aside. Put the oxtail in the heated potjie, add the toasted spices and brown the meat, then add the chicken stock, peppercorns, fennel bulbs and white wine. Add the sautéed vegetables and some pepper to taste, and gently simmer over a medium heat until the meat is soft – about 4 hours.

While the oxtail is slowly simmering away, wrap the potatoes in tinfoil and place next to the coals. When they are cooked through, make the Stilton gnocchi by following the instructions on page 66. Simply add the blue cheese after mashing the potatoes.

About 40 minutes before the oxtail is cooked, add the peeled whole pears – make sure you don't stir the potjie during this stage otherwise you'll end up with mushed up pears.

Spoon out some of that lovely fat that's been gathering at the top of your oxtail pot and drizzle into a hot pan. Add the gnocchi in batches and fry for a couple of minutes until golden. Finally, place the golden gnocchi on top of the oxtail just before you're going to eat and mix together a quick gremolata to sprinkle over the top.

GREMOLATA: Chop together 1 handful of fresh parsley, the zest of 1 lemon and 2 cloves garlic. Great to cut through all that fattiness of the oxtail or any fatty meat dish.

spiced TEA

BY *Bertus Basson*

1 enamel kettle

1 litre water

1 orange

1 lemon

3–4 tablespoons of Rooibos
tea leaves

2 vanilla pods

1 cinnamon stick

1 stalk lemongrass, bruised
and halved

about 1 tablespoon of green
cardamom pods

about 2 tablespoons of sugar

a shot of KWV 10-year-old
brandy

1 large glass jar

muslin cloth

This tea will warm you up from the inside out on those cold
winter nights when the African TV is just not doing the trick.

Pour 1 litre of water into an enamel kettle. Slice the orange and
the lemon in half, then squeeze the juice of both into the water.
Add the tea, whole vanilla pods, cinnamon stick, lemongrass,
cardamom and stir in the sugar to taste (the 2 tablespoons should
do the trick, but adjust to your own liking). Next, add a shot or two
of brandy, put the lid onto the kettle and place over moderate to
hot coals. Let the tea simmer and infuse for about 10 minutes – it
should be done when it has reached boiling point. Tie some muslin
cloth around the mouth of the glass jar and slowly pour the tea
into the jar. Serve the entire jar to a thirsty friend, or divide into
four cups.

APRICOT MALVA WITH
Brandy Glaze

After spending so many years in the big smoke of London, Petrus was excited to make a big malva pudding with an apricot twist. If you're not a fan of dried fruit, make this pudding without it. And if you want to experiment using different kinds of dried fruit, then go ahead and do that. Half the fun of cooking is trying different ingredients and seeing what you like best. Whatever you decide to do is up to you, but stick to the exact quantities listed below. Baking is a science and if you deviate from the rules, chances are that you'll end up with a disaster.

FOR THE PUDDING:

1 cup of brown sugar

2 eggs

2 tablespoons of apricot jam

1½ cups of cake flour

a pinch of salt

2 teaspoons of bicarbonate of soda

2 tablespoons of butter

1 teaspoon of white wine vinegar

½ cup of milk

½ cup of dried apricots, chopped

FOR THE GLAZE:

1 big knob of butter

½ cup of sugar

1 cup of fresh cream

½ cup of KWV brandy

For the pudding, beat the sugar and eggs in a bowl until the mixture is smooth and fluffy, then stir through the apricot jam and set aside.

In a separate bowl, sift together the flour, salt and bicarbonate of soda. Melt the butter, wait for it to cool slightly, then mix with the white wine vinegar and the milk. Add the flour mixture and combine thoroughly, folding as you go. Stir in half of the chopped apricots and set the pudding batter aside.

Take some butter and grease a flat-bottom potjie. Pour in the batter and place the potjie on a grid over moderate coals, with a scattering of coals over the lid. Bake the pudding for 45–60 minutes – when it's golden on top and if you stick a knife or skewer through the centre of the pudding and it comes out clean, it's ready.

To make the brandy glaze, simply melt the butter and sugar, stir through the cream and add the other half of the apricots and the brandy and keep warm until the pudding is ready. While the pudding is still nice and hot, pour the glaze over the top. Serve immediately with lashings of double-thick whipped cream or really good vanilla ice cream. (Make your own ice cream! Check out page 153 to see how to do this.)

PS: When I make malva pudding in the oven, I like to do it in a muffin tray so everyone gets their own little portion... and it bakes faster. So if you want to, do that instead.

BY *Petrus Madutlela*

This place might as well be called ISOLATION, because that's exactly what it is. The last stretch into Noup felt eerie… once we managed to get through security that is. It took some convincing that we were not lost, but actually there on purpose. The security guy seemed completely flabbergasted that we had chosen Noup as one of the best off-the-beaten track destinations. But once we managed to convince him, we got back on the road. Which was very (very) straight. And narrow. And long – it'll take about an hour to drive it so if you're tired, let your buddy take over. If you fall asleep at the wheel and crash your car, chances are that you will never, ever be found. Driving that road felt a little surreal and there's a strange energy – it's not something I can explain, but this is the kind of stuff that we live for… just so we can exaggerate and tell stories about it later.

Noup (just outside the 700-square kilometre Namaqua National Park) is not a top-travel destination, which is exactly why we travelled there – *that* and the fact that with more than half the crew being Capetonians, we can never stay away from the ocean for too long… and after our visit here it would be a while before we would get to smell the ocean again.

The thing that makes Noup so special (and deserted) is that it forms part of the wild and rugged West Coast that has been dominated on one hand by the merciless African sun that's been baking this hard earth for thousands of years, and on the other hand it's got the wild Atlantic Ocean that's been pounding into these shores with Herculean persistence – leaving a scattering of diamonds and shipwrecks along the coastline. Which brings me to the Diamond Diver Cottages, the perfect destination for the road tripper who is seeking solace and an escape from the rat race – with the bonus of unspoilt, panoramic views of the ocean. These cottages were built and lived in by diamond divers back in 1989 and when the diamonds were depleted the divers left… In times of old this area was not for the faint-hearted traveller… and probably still isn't today.

THE FAR SIDE

NO DRIVING ON BEACH

SALAD BRO!

Josh used to work in Bertus's kitchen until he got fired for always giving Bertus lip. Kidding. He quit – he couldn't handle Bertus shouting at him all the time. Still kidding. We're actually not sure why he left, but he ended up with us on the road anyway! And when he spent an afternoon making three different salads for the crew chilling next to the Bulshoek Dam, we were happy he was there. Sometimes (and especially when you work on a show that deals with a lot of meat-eating and -braaiing, a fresh, flavourful and tasty salad is juuust what you need.) Thanks Josh!

BY Josh Wiid

Slaw

Finely slice all the veggies that need to be sliced and place in a large bowl. Now you're going to make your own mayonnaise. By yourself. From scratch. First up, whisk the mustard into the egg yolks, then in a slow and steady stream whisk in the oil. This will take a bit of effort, but the difference in taste when you make your own mayo is huge. To make it a little easier, Josh says to put the bowl onto a damp cloth, that way freeing up both hands for whisking and pouring. Keep whisking until the oil has been incorporated and the mayo is nice and thick. If you feel brave, turn the bowl upside down over your head. If nothing falls onto said head, then you're good to go. If it does... sorry about that!

Season to taste and add a decent squeeze of lemon juice – have a taste and adjust to your liking. Add the cream cheese a couple of dollops at a time, and whisk until smooth. Combine the mayo and the slaw, then garnish with the pea shoots, another squeeze of lemon and a pinch of salt.

YOU NEED:

1 medium white cabbage, finely sliced

1 medium red cabbage, finely sliced

2 big handfuls of radishes, thinly sliced

8 baby turnips, halved and sliced

½ cup of fennel, finely sliced or dill tops

2 tablespoons of Dijon mustard

7 free-range egg yolks

about 2 cups of canola oil

salt and pepper to taste

juice of ½ lemon

1 cup of plain cream cheese

2 big handfuls of pea shoots for garnishing

Zesty Potato Salad

This is a fresh variation on the usual mayonnaise-drenched potato salad that we serve up with almost every braai in summer. Give it a bash!

YOU NEED:

about 1 kg baby potatoes, cooked and halved

½ cup of wholegrain mustard

zest of 3 lemons and 3 oranges, and the juice of 1 of each

salt to taste

1 small handful of fresh parsley, chopped

micro-herbs for garnishing

While the potatoes are cooking, combine the mustard, zest, juice and salt to taste. Don't worry if it tastes too acidic – the potatoes will balance out the flavours. Once the potatoes are cooked and halved, and while they're still hot, put them in a big bowl, and stir through the mustard vinaigrette. Pop into the fridge for 1 hour and allow the flavours to develop. Garnish with fresh parsley and micro-herbs and serve with your favourite braaied meat.

Candied Sweet Potato

Ok, this isn't really a salad. In fact, it's a combination of baked pudding married to baked sweet potato. But it's still great as a side with *braaivleis*, and Josh learned how to make this from Bertus a couple of years ago, and it's sinfully delicious.

YOU NEED:

about 10 sweet potatoes, cooked

1½ cups of butter

1 bottle of maple syrup

a pinch of salt

about 2 cups of toasted pecan nuts, crushed

Once you've cooked the sweet potatoes until soft but not mushy, cut them into 5-cm thick rounds and set aside. Melt the butter in a large, fireproof saucepan over moderate to cool coals, then slowly stir in the syrup and salt until combined. Warning: If the coals are too hot, the butter will burn, and if you add the syrup too quickly it will split. Once combined, simmer very gently to reduce and darken in colour. While that's on the go, take the sweet potato rounds and pop them into a large pan to grill and caramelise on both sides. Once the sweet potatoes are charred, pour the hot caramel over them and simmer for about 5 minutes a side, continuously basting with excess caramel from the pan. Remove from the heat, sprinkle over the crushed pecan nuts and serve.

You are about to make your friends very happy!

85

Games
People Play

We are definitely not all work and no play. We know how to keep the balance – this is what keeps us sane. So if you ever find yourself in the middle of nowhere, here are some games that should keep you entertained for a couple of hours. I'll explain the less obvious ones.

HACKY SACK

This is probably the most popular game when we're on the road and has become a bit of a tradition thanks to Robbie (our Content Director). For some reason it's usually only played by the guys, and chances are that when the convoy pulls over to do some leg stretching, you'll soon see a group of four or five of them standing in a circle, kicking the hacky sack to each other. The object of the game is to keep the 'hack' in the air and to pass it from player to player without dropping it or touching it with your hands. It's pretty much the same as playing bounce... but without a soccer ball and without any bounces. When it comes to the rules, it gets a little complicated – especially because there are Durban rules, Cape Town rules and Joburg rules – but the basic ones are:

1. No self-service (in other words, this is a group game, not a solo adventure... so pass the hack!).

2. No catching the hack (unless it's about to hit an unsuspecting passer-by... but then again, maybe just let it hit them for extra entertainment value).

3. No hack abuse (that means, don't stand on the hack – that's just rude).

4. The hack can't go through your legs.

5. You're not allowed to say the word 'sorry' (barbarians!).

If you break any of the rules you have to turn around and take one for the team (in other words, get the hack thrown at your back by another player).

SHITHEAD

This is a really fun card game (especially if you win) and the idea is that you have to get rid of your cards as fast as possible... the person left at the end with cards is the shithead... and *no one* wants to be that.

To play you need two packs of cards and between four and eight friends. (If you're only four people playing, you'll only need one pack of cards). Remove the Jokers from the pack and shuffle the two packs together. Each player gets three cards, placed face-down (no one is allowed to see what these cards are). Deal three face-up cards on top of the three face-down cards. Then deal three cards to each player that they keep in their hands. If they want to, players can switch cards in their hand with their face-up cards should it help them produce a strong set of 'face-up' cards for later in the game. The remaining pack goes face-down into the middle of the game. The first player with a three in their hand starts the game by placing it on the discard pile, then the game continues in a clockwise direction. If no one has a three, then the person with a four starts, and if no one has a four, the next logical number would be five. You get the picture...

THE RULES:

1. Each player must put down a card (or more if they have them) of the same number or higher than the one at the top of the discard pile. (So if the card on the pile is a 4 for example, and you have three 5s in your hand, you can play all three, but then your turn is over.)

2. The game continues in a clockwise direction until a 'change direction card' is played.

3. Each player must have three cards in their hand at all times, until the pick-up pile has been depleted.

4. If you can't play a card, you have to take the entire discard pile and put it in your hand, then end your turn.

5. When you have no more cards in your hand, and the pick-up pile is empty, it's time to start playing with your three face-up cards on the table. The same rule applies here that should you be unable to play a card equal to or higher than the one on the discard pile, you have to pick up that pile and put it in your hand.

6. When you've played all the cards in your hand, as well as your face-up cards, then it's time to play your face-down cards (also known as the 'blind cards'). No peeking!

7. The same rule applies yet again – if a card from the blind pile is not equal or higher than the one in the discard pile, it's time to pick up the entire discard pile again.

8. If you're able to complete a set in one turn, for example, complete four-of-kind threes, you clear (or burn) the entire pile from play. You can play another card immediately after 'burning' the pile.

9. The first player with no more cards left to play is the winner. The rest of the group continues to play until there is only one player left. That unlucky player then becomes the shithead. And usually the poor sod who has to buy everyone another round of drinks.

SPECIAL CARDS

These cards can be played on any card, no matter what its value:

2: Playing this card allows the next player to play any card in his or her hand.

10: This burns the pile and removes it from the game. And remember if you burn a pile, you get to play a card immediately after.

3: Changes direction of play.

5: Mirrors the card previously played. So if it's played on a 3, then it becomes a 3.

7: The next player must match the 7 or go lower.

8: Playing an 8 means the next player misses their turn.

Kick a Soccer Ball At Someone

You need at least six people to play this game. And a soccer ball. And maybe a helmet if you're feeling kind. This is a bit like dodge ball, except there's only one victim at a time. Get them to sit in the middle of the circle (the radius needs to be fairly large). Everyone gets a turn to kick the ball until the person (okay, victim) in the middle is hit by the ball. Then swop out with a player and start again. Admittedly, this game is very childish, and I never took part in it. But a lot of the younger crew did. Each to their own I suppose.

Guess the Story

Gather between four and six friends and get comfortable at a table. A cold bucket of beer is strongly recommended.

Get two sheets of paper and two pens.

Give a sheet of paper to two people.

They now have to write down a sentence without showing anyone what they've written. It can be anything, for example 'The cat sat on a hot tin roof' or 'The kid on the bicycle injured himself after cycling into a tree' – go wild and use your imagination.

Get the two people who wrote the sentences to pass the paper onto the person sitting to their left. These two people now draw a picture that illustrates that sentence. They now have to fold the paper over the sentence, but still show the picture. The paper gets passed to the left again. The next two people now have to write a sentence that will explain what the picture is, and fold the paper so that the picture is now hidden, and only their sentence can be seen. Keep alternating between writing and drawing until the paper ends up with the original creator, who gets to reveal what everyone thought they saw or tried to illustrate. The results are always hilarious and it's a fun way to kill some time.

If none of these games appeal to you, then just take along a pack of cards and board games (chess, 30 Seconds, Scrabble, Monopoly etc). When you have time to kill or you're feeling a little restless, you'll be happy that you did.

SPICY
Chicken Wings
BY Bertus Basson

FOR THE WINGS:

at least 4 free-range chicken wings per friend... so go count them

metal or bamboo skewers

lime wedges for serving

FOR THE BASTING SAUCE:

about 4 chillies (or more), seeded and finely chopped

about 6 tablespoons of sugar

juice of 1 lemon

2 cups of tomato sauce

about 1 handful of fresh coriander, finely chopped

3 cloves garlic, crushed

salt and pepper to taste

What's not to love about spicy wings? It's the perfect excuse to eat with your hands, lick your fingers, suck on some bones and to have a bucket of beers chilling on ice at your table. This is guy food at its best.

First up, clean and prepare the chicken wings. Next, if you're going to use bamboo skewers, submerge them in water and soak while you get on with the rest of the prep.

Combine all the sauce ingredients, pour over the chicken wings, cover and leave for about 1 hour.

When the coals are moderate (and the guys are starting to misbehave) get those babies onto skewers and start braaiing. If you want to you can skewer the chicken first and then pour the marinade over – up to you! (A lot of people stretch the wings out when skewering, which does help to crisp up the skin, but Bertus says it's better to keep them in their natural shape to ensure that the chicken doesn't dry out.)

Keep turning and basting the wings until the skin is nice and crispy and the chicken is completely cooked – 25–30 minutes. Serve with Slaw (page 82), Zesty Potato Salad (page 84) and some Mealie Bread (page 92).

BR

Mealie BREAD

YOU NEED:

3 cups of self-raising flour

½ cup of creamed sweetcorn

½ cup of whole kernel corn

1 cup of buttermilk

3 eggs, whisked

1 cup of grated Parmesan cheese

2 tablespoons of brown sugar

a pinch of salt

2 tablespoons of butter

maize meal for dusting

BY *Petrus Madutlela*

This is a South African classic rooted in our grandmothers' kitchens! Have it with lashings of butter or give it an Asian twist and make a Chicken Satay Sarmie (page 94) like Bertus and Petrus did in Noup.

Put the flour into a large mixing bowl and then add the sweetcorn, corn kernels, buttermilk, whisked eggs, cheese, sugar and salt. Mix thoroughly with a wooden spoon in a folding motion until properly combined, and then set aside. Take either a flat-bottom potjie or a cast-iron bread pot and use the butter to grease the bottom and sides. Dust with maize meal and scrape the dough into the pot, then put the lid on. Place the bread over moderate to cool coals, put a few coals on the lid to create an oven effect and bake for about 40 minutes or until the bread is golden. The best way to test if it's cooked all the way through is to stick a skewer or butter knife into the centre of the bread, and if it comes out clean the bread is ready. Allow to cool slightly before turning it out onto a wooden board, and leave for about 10 minutes before slicing.

**For about 6 people,
YOU NEED:**

1 handful of peanuts

1 disk of palm sugar

*1 stalk of lemongrass, bruised
and chopped*

zest and juice of 1 lime

a couple of chillies, halved

*1 big chunk of fresh ginger,
finely chopped*

about 2 teaspoons of peanut oil

1 tablespoon of fish sauce

*1 handful of Parmesan
shavings*

1 x 400 ml tin coconut milk

*1 handful of fresh coriander,
chopped*

1 lime, halved

5 deboned chicken legs

5 deboned chicken thighs

SLAW:

½ red cabbage, shredded

*about 5 radishes, very thinly
sliced*

*1 handful of fresh coriander,
chopped*

½ onion, finely chopped

your favourite micro-herbs

Chicken Satay & SARMIES

BY *Bertus & Petrus*

Start by making the satay in a mortar and pestle. Bash together the peanuts, palm sugar, lemongrass, lime zest and juice, chillies, ginger and peanut oil. Next, add the fish sauce and Parmesan shavings and bash it some more. Scrape the mixture into a large bowl, then stir in the coconut milk and fresh coriander. Pour about three-quarters of the sauce over the deboned chicken and let it marinate for at least 1 hour. (If you can leave it in the fridge overnight, even better.) Keep the rest of the sauce to use later.

When your coals are at a moderate heat, place the marinated chicken inside a sandwich grid and braai for about 20 minutes (or until cooked through), basting with the satay sauce as you go.

Mix together all the slaw ingredients. Arrange the chicken satay on top of slices of fresh Mealie Bread (page 92). Top each with a handful of slaw and drizzle with the extra satay sauce you set aside. Eat these open-sandwich style.

FABER'S
Famous Crew Chicken

YOU NEED:

2 spatchcocked chickens... AND THEN

2 basting brushes

2 sandwich braai grids

FOR BBQ CHICKEN:

Simply mix together 2½ cups of tomato sauce, 4 tablespoons of brown sugar, a couple of splashes of Worcestershire sauce, 3 tablespoons each of white spirit vinegar and Dijon mustard, and a dash of cayenne pepper. Simmer for 30 minutes and you're ready to braai.

FOR EASY PERI-PERI:

1 bottle of Nando's Peri-Peri sauce (yes, really)

juice of 2 lemons

a couple of chillies, chopped

a couple of cloves garlic, crushed and chopped

salt and pepper to taste

Some traditions start taking shape when you spend too much time together. One that stands out as a definite favourite amongst the crew was when Andrew would raid the Pick n Pay truck for a braai on our days off. You'd think that when you work on a braai show 24/7 you would start to get sick of it, but the exact opposite is true. This braai always happened after lunchtime, with his car boot open, music blaring from the speakers and he would have his second drink in his hand. Like I said... tradition – and in this case a very South African one.

While he braaied many things, the most popular was the chicken – one peri-peri and the other BBQ. These were served with nothing else. Just perfectly braaied chicken cut and eaten straight off the grid to tide us over until dinner on those lekker long lazy days. This is not fancy. It's, in fact, extremely simple. But still delicious

Place your spatchcocked chicken in between sandwich grids. Place (bone-side first) over moderate coals then braai and baste the birds with the different sauces. Flip them over every 10 minutes and baste again. The chicken should be cooked through to the bone and the flesh crispy after about 40 minutes. You'll know they're ready when you stick a knife through the thickest part and the juices run clear.

NAMIBIA...

It was finally time to cross the border into Namibia, but before we did that we stopped off in Springbok (a small town in the middle of nowhere) to stock up on supplies. This is important because once you're in Namibia, and especially if you go off-the-beaten-track, it's hard to get even the simplest things. And so we stocked up on stuff like beers, wine, biltong and anything we thought we wouldn't be able to get our hands on once in Namibia.

The first important thing to remember when you're going to cross the border is that you're only allowed to take a certain amount of things over – alcohol is an example – and if you're in excess, you'll either get a big fat fine or it will be confiscated by the officials. It's not worth taking the risk. Another tip? ALWAYS be friendly to the border officials. They're like the kids who never got elected as prefects, so they like the power game. And even if you feel your ears burning red-hot and you want to tell them off for being so damn rude, don't. Grin and bear it – they can make your life and border-crossing-experience absolute hell. On that note, you need to be prepared, and in order to get into Namibia, this is what you need to know:

BORDER TIMES:

1. Vioolsdrift to Noordoewer. Open 24 hours.

2. Alexander Bay to Oranjemund. Open 6 a.m. to 10 p.m.

3. Sendelingsdrift. 8 a.m. to 5 p.m.

4. Onseepkans to Vellorsdrift. 8 a.m. to 5 p.m.

5. Nakop to Ariamsvlei. Open 24 hours.

6. Rietfontein to Klein Menasse. 8 a.m. to 4:30 p.m.

IN YOUR TRAVEL BAG...

A Passport – with at least four blank pages. The passport should be valid for at least six months from the exact date you leave South Africa.

A Driver's Licence – this is valid in Namibia and will be accepted at the border.

Cash – To pay the road user's fee. Bring extra if you have a trailer. Also handy to have cash on hand for bribes...

ZA Sticker – Get these at any AA sales agent.

Vehicle Papers – This one is a bit of admin, but if your car documents are not in order you won't be allowed to cross over. And then you would feel sad. So get the following: Proof of ownership (either vehicle owner or rental company). Go to your nearest 'popo' and get a Police Clearance Certificate. Remember that the engine number, chassis, trailer number (if you have one) and licence details will be checked by the police at the border post. Go to the bank to get a letter giving you authorisation to take the vehicle over the border (make sure they include dates). All these letters need to be signed by the Commissioner of Oaths.

Letter of Authority – only applicable if you're travelling in a rental car. No police clearance necessary for this.

HURRAH! I MADE IT ACROSS. NOW WHAT?

The first thing you'll notice when you get into Namibia is how quickly the landscape changes. You'll feel like you've just landed on a different planet. So slow down and breathe it all in. And while you're doing that, and if it's between April and September, set your watch back by an hour.

Although the roads in Namibia are mostly in good nick, I'd recommend travelling in a 4x4 – especially if you're going to travel to the places we did. I also recommend driving slowly with the windows open. Keep an eye open for animals crossing the road and if you happen to go through a farm gate, make sure you close it. Also, get your hands on a Namibian sim-card for your phone – even though reception is bad and you'll probably never have signal, it's good to have it in case of an emergency. On that note... Namibia, with only two million people, is a large and remote country and places are few and far between, so make sure to fill up at petrol stations whenever you can – even if your tank is almost full. Other than that, the only advice I can give you is to have fun, stick to the speed limit, keep your eyes open and get lost in this painted landscape.

ORANGE

E RIVER

Our first stop in Namibia was a place that sits firmly in my heart: the Felix Unite Provenance Camp on the banks of one of the mightiest rivers in Africa: the Orange River. I've come here many times and every time I do, and no matter how many times I sit on the banks of this river, I can't be anything but mesmerised. I think this is one of the most beautiful places in the world.

From the Orange River's source in the Mountain Kingdom of Lesotho, she carves her way for about 2 000 kilometres through parts of southern Africa right down to her mouth at Alexander Bay near the Skeleton Coast. Although her course might be ancient, on her banks and away into the interior – away from her life-giving force – the landscape has been beautifully sculpted by wind and water erosion, providing evidence of nature's power. In a sense you feel dwarfed by the sheer scale and scope of this land.

River aside, Felix Unite is one of the best places to put up your feet and relax... which is exactly what we did for two days before getting back to the business of filming. And while some of us opted to catch up with our families, laze around and spend some time getting back in touch with ourselves, a few others decided to do a two-day trip down the river to escape the travel circus. These are the kind of things we have to do every now and then to stay sane on the road... especially since we were only halfway on our trip. And that's the beauty of properly planning your trip – when you do, you get to experience so much more.

Wet & Dry Rubs

Choosing when to make a wet rub or a dry rub is up to you – either way you're enhancing the natural flavour of the meat. A dry rub is just that – a combination of spices and herbs that work well together. Use a dry rub on meat that you're going to braai quickly over a high heat. While there are no real rules to making a dry rub, try to stick to what you know will work. The one opposite is Bertus's rub for beef and it's really simple and tasty. If you want, quadruple the quantities of herbs and spices and store it in a jar for every time you have a steak begging to be braaied.

A wet rub is when you add liquid to a dry rub. *That* simple. This is the best rub for slow cooking or long marinating times – think ribs and chicken. The consistency of the rub is up to you (from paste-like to saucy) – as long as it sticks to the meat.

WET RUB BY Petrus

for Asian-Style Beef Fillet Skewers

100 ml soy sauce

2 tablespoons of grated fresh ginger

a splash of fish sauce

a pinch of sugar

2 cloves garlic, crushed

1 chilli, sliced (seeds and all)

a splash of cola

3 tablespoons of olive oil

a squeeze of lemon juice

½ stalk lemongrass, finely chopped

a pinch of salt

fillet

1 garlic bulb, sliced in half and roasted over the coals

extra lemongrass to use as skewers

Mix together all the wet rub ingredients, except the halved garlic and the whole lemongrass, in a large bowl. Next, cube the fillet into equal sizes then mix them through the wet rub until evenly coated. Pop into the fridge for 30–60 minutes – the longer it marinates, the better.

In the meantime, roast some garlic straight on the braai grid over low coals – be careful not to burn it!

Peel off any brown leaves, then cut the lemongrass into small skewers. Make a small incision in each piece of fillet then thread two to three cubes onto each lemongrass skewer and set aside.

Cook the meat, and try to turn it three times at most to ensure it keeps all that lovely moisture. While the meat is on the braai, use the halved roasted garlic, dunk it into the leftover marinade and baste the fillet with it often.

Braai until done to your liking, then remove from the heat. Leave to rest for at least 5 minutes before serving.

BY *Bertus*

DRY RUB
for Beef Fillet

2 tablespoons of coarse salt

2 tablespoons of sugar

¾ tablespoon of Robertsons ground coriander

¾ tablespoon of Robertsons ground allspice

1 tablespoon of Robertsons paprika

½ tablespoon of Robertsons cayenne pepper

fillet

a couple of sprigs of fresh thyme, leaves stripped off

3 cloves garlic, sliced

Mix together all the ingredients, then rub it all over your steaks. Leave for at least 1 hour before cooking. Braai over a hot fire until medium-rare (or to however you like it, but anything over medium is sacrilege). Let the meat rest for at least 5 minutes before slicing.

TIP: Contrary to popular belief, Bertus says you should season your meat before you braai it. But don't use fine salt – it penetrates the meat too quickly and then you might have overly salty steak – not so lekker. Stick to coarse salt.

Down River, DOWN RIVER

Paddling down the Orange River is something you need to put on your bucket list. Even if you've done it before, do it again. Here are a few things to expect when you're on the river:

1. Chances are good that you're going to capsize at some point, so make sure you've got extra dry clothes in your bucket. And that you're wearing a swimsuit. And that you know how to swim.

2. Choose your paddling buddy very carefully – you're going to be on a kayak with them for 40-odd kilometres.

3. Drinking and paddling is allowed. In fact, it's highly recommended. Just make sure that you follow every beer you have with some water. Not river water... the drinking kind.

4. Wear a hat. Even if you're river-venturing in winter, protection from the sun is *always* a good idea. Pack a warm jacket for the night, and decanter some liquid gold into a plastic bottle to enjoy around the African TV.

5. Listen to the river guide. Except when he says that the end of the paddle is just around the corner. He's lying. It's *never* just around the next bend.

6. Know the rules of the oars on the water. And *especially* on the banks of the river. When the oar is horizontal, it means the 'toilet area' is occupied. Vertical? Safe to go!

7. Take a sleeping bag and a makeshift pillow (small enough to fit into your bucket). You're going to sleep right on the banks of the river. Next to a huge bonfire. Under a gazillion stars. It's going to be the best sleep you've ever had, guaranteed.

8. Forget about time. That's the beauty of a trip like this. And I promise you, you're going to have one of the best adventures you'll ever have.

9. Take some snacks. If you're feeling kind, share these with the friends that were stupid enough to forget their own.

10. Leave it as you found it so that everyone else can enjoy it too. Don't be k*k.

Robertsons Spice Combos

To make the following spices, simply combine them and store them in airtight jars in your kitchen. They're handy to have and it's quite cool to make your own combinations.

CHINESE FIVE-SPICE

4 tablespoons of ground star anise

2 tablespoons of ground black pepper

2 tablespoons of ground fennel

2 tablespoons of ground cinnamon

2 tablespoons of ground cloves

2 tablespoons of coarse sea salt

DUKKAH

½ cup of toasted nuts, crushed

½ cup of toasted sesame seeds

2 tablespoons of coriander seeds, toasted

2 tablespoons of cumin seeds, toasted

2 teaspoons of ground black pepper

1 teaspoon of flaked sea salt

CAJUN SPICE

4 tablespoons of paprika

2 tablespoons of coarse sea salt

2 tablespoons of ground black pepper

2 tablespoons of cayenne pepper

2 tablespoons of mustard powder

CHICKEN SPICE

2½ tablespoons of coarse sea salt

1 tablespoon of dried basil

1 tablespoon of dried rosemary

2 teaspoons of garlic powder

2 teaspoons of mustard powder

2 teaspoons of paprika

2 teaspoons of ground black pepper

2 teaspoons of dried thyme

1 teaspoon of dried parsley

½ teaspoon of ground cumin

½ teaspoon of cayenne pepper

FISH SPICE

1 tablespoon of dried basil

1 tablespoon of dried rosemary

1 tablespoon of dried parsley

2½ teaspoons of coarse sea salt

2½ teaspoons of dried sage

2½ teaspoons of dried thyme

2½ teaspoons of dried marjoram

1 teaspoon of dried oregano

1 teaspoon of celery salt

1 teaspoon of garlic powder

JAMAICAN JERK

1 tablespoon of onion flakes

1 tablespoon of garlic powder

2 teaspoons of dried thyme

2 teaspoons of coarse sea salt

2 teaspoons of sugar

1 teaspoon of dried parsley

1 teaspoon of ground allspice

½ teaspoon of cayenne pepper

½ teaspoon of dried chilli flakes

¼ teaspoon of ground cinnamon

¼ teaspoon of ground cumin

¼ teaspoon of ground nutmeg

• • • • • • • • • • • • • • • • • • •

HERBS DE PROVENCE

2 tablespoons of dried rosemary

2 tablespoons of dried thyme

2 tablespoons of dried basil

2 tablespoons of dried marjoram

2 tablespoons of dried lavender flowers

2 tablespoons of dried parsley

1 tablespoon of fennel seeds

1 tablespoon of dried oregano

1 tablespoon of dried tarragon

1 tablespoon of crushed bay leaves

GREEK

2 tablespoons of coarse sea salt

2 tablespoons of garlic powder

2 tablespoons of dried basil

2 tablespoons of dried oregano

1 tablespoon of ground cinnamon

1 tablespoon of ground black pepper

1 tablespoon of dried parsley

1 tablespoon of dried rosemary

1 tablespoon of dried dill

1 tablespoon of dried marjoram

1 teaspoon of dried thyme

1 teaspoon of ground nutmeg

• • • • • • • • • • • • • • • • • • •

ITALIAN

3 tablespoons of dried basil

3 tablespoons of dried marjoram

3 tablespoons of dried oregano

1½ tablespoons of dried thyme

1½ tablespoons of dried rosemary

A few words from Cass Abrahams, renowned chef and spice lover, on her favourite spices.

Cumin: Warm and earthy. Use in curries.

Allspice: When you bite into it, you taste many different spices. When used with peppercorns and cloves it becomes the 'Holy Trinity' of a good potjie or stew.

Garlic: Don't fry it in oil. Rather add it to liquid – this way it releases its natural sweetness the way it's meant to.

Mustard seeds: Fry in oil until the seeds have popped.

Fenugreek: This is a great spice to use in vegetable dishes – but don't use too much. Add a very tiny pinch and it will bring out the natural sweetness in vegetables and you will taste each individual veggie.

Cloves: Tends to be very strong but add two or three whole cloves to rice or biryani.

Smiler's
SWEET & SOUR
Sticky Ribs

Ribs that'll make you smile from ear to ear to ear to ear!

For 4 kg of free-range pork ribs

FOR THE BRINE:

6 litres chicken stock

6 tablespoons of honey

6 tablespoons of red wine vinegar

6 tablespoons of soy sauce

6 tablespoons of ponzu sauce (available at most Asian supermarkets)

3 tablespoons of oyster sauce

FOR THE BASTING SAUCE:

1 chunk of ginger

4 cloves garlic

4 tablespoons of oyster sauce

6 tablespoons of each soy sauce, ponzu sauce, red wine vinegar and honey

½ bottle of peach chutney

2 cups of cola

The first thing you're going to do is to get all the brine ingredients in a big cast-iron pot, then pop the ribs inside. Place the pot over moderate coals and bring to a simmer for about 45 minutes or until the meat is tender (but not falling off the bones!). Take the pot off the coals and let the ribs rest in the brine while you make the basting sauce.

Put all the ingredients in a fireproof pan over moderate coals and reduce until the basting sauce is nice and sticky – similar to the consistency of caramel. Have a taste and adjust the sauce until you have just the right balance of sweet and sour flavours. If it's too sweet, add more vinegar, or too sour, add more honey.

Remove the ribs from the brine and place in a large *braai-bak*, then pour all that lovely sauce over them and keep to the side until you're ready to braai.

Braai the ribs over moderate coals for about 15 minutes, turning them often and brushing with basting sauce to turn them into finger-licking, perfectly sticky ribs.

Stuffed MASCARPONE Potatoes

BY *Yusuf & Stephen*

YOU NEED:

1 potato per friend

tinfoil

coarse salt

FOR THE FILLING:

1 x 250 g tub mascarpone cheese

zest and juice of 1 lemon

2 tablespoons of capers, chopped

½ garlic bulb, roasted

1 handful of chives, chopped

a glug of olive oil

½ red onion, finely chopped

salt and pepper to taste

butter

This is a really simple and delicious side that will work with any type of braaivleis.

Place each potato on a piece of tinfoil, season with coarse salt and wrap up. Place the wrapped potatoes around low coals and cook until soft. About 10 minutes before they're going to be done, make the filling. Simply mix together the ingredients, except the butter, and season to taste. When the potatoes are cooked through, slice them down the middle, add butter and then the cheese mixture. Squeeze the potatoes together to secure.

BY *PJ Vades*

PJ'S PORK BELLY

Thank the lard for men like PJ Vades. He is the go-to guy for all things pork, and we were lucky enough to have him join us on the road. Even better than that, he made a delicious rolled pork belly for those lucky enough to be in his vicinity to enjoy. If you don't know who PJ is, all you need to know is that he is the King of Pork and is actually in the process of opening his own porker spot in Cape Town, so if you're ever in the area, go find it. If not, then just try his rolled pork belly recipe. The result will put a smile on your face, three times. The first time is when you cut into the belly and you hear that beautiful crunch of the crackling on the outside. The second time will be when you actually taste that crackling – this is the food of the gods. And the third time you'll smile and nod in appreciation is when you taste the pork itself – perfectly tender, juicy and flavourful meat that will melt in your mouth.

MEET THE BIG GREEN EGG:

Sounds a little like Green Eggs And Ham, but it's not that. Although you could roast some ham inside of one if you wanted to. The Big Green Egg has changed the way I braai a lot of things, and it's not just me. Bertus now uses them at his restaurant too and has mastered the art of the Big Green Egg – cooking on three at the same time! The big bonus of the Big Green Egg is its consistent heat control, which gives me more time to kuier with my mates while the food is on the go. I just put whatever I'm braaiing inside, close her up and walk away until the food is cooked. As much as I'm a fan of cooking over the open fire, I'm also a fan of sometimes not having to sweat over one for an entire day.

FIRST THINGS FIRST:

Go get your hands on a free-range pork belly. If the ribs are still attached, that's no problem – they're easy to remove and make for another tasty pork dish to grease up your chin.

1. Remove the ribs from the belly by cutting closely along the bones, until you've removed them completely. Keep the baby back ribs for another day.

2. Check for excess cartilage along the edge of the belly and cut that off too.

3. Using a sharp knife, score the skin side of the belly then rub coarse sea salt into the skin and leave in the fridge overnight – this helps to make that perfect crispy crackling.

FOR THE BRINE:

1 litre water

200 g sugar

200 g salt

1 bunch of fresh rosemary sprigs

1 bunch of fresh thyme

about 8 cloves garlic, kept whole

FOR THE RUB:

20 g fennel seeds

20 g cumin seeds

20 g juniper berries

1 deboned free-range pork belly

coarse salt

Make the brine the day before you're going to roast the belly. This will allow the flavours to fully develop. Bring the water to the boil over moderate coals, then add the sugar and salt and stir to dissolve. Next add the herbs and garlic and continue to simmer for about 10 minutes, then remove from the heat and allow to cool. Pour the brine into a container and let it sleep next to your pork belly overnight.

Dry-toast the spices in a nonstick pan over moderate coals until fragrant. Remove from the heat and then crush them in a mortar and pestle.

Place the pork belly on a clean surface so that the flesh-side is facing up. First season with salt and then generously rub the spice mix onto the flesh.

Now it's time to roll up the belly – and PJ says the best way to do this is to do it from the thick side to the thin side, so best you do that seeing that he's *the* expert. Once rolled up, grab some butcher's string and tie up the belly in a twist and loop motion, lengthways, until secured. Pop the belly into a roasting tin and inject it with the brine at intervals.

Once the thermometer on your Big Green Egg says the temperature is at 180 °C, pop the belly inside and close the lid. The meat has to roast for 3 hours, but unfortunately you can't just walk away from it and leave it because you need to inject it with the leftover brine to keep it moist, and you need to turn the belly every 20–30 minutes. And it will be absolutely worth it when you taste it. After 3 hours you should have the perfect, crispy on the outside, moist on the inside, rolled pork belly, so remove from the heat and place on a wooden board. Cut the string off the belly – don't worry, it will stay intact without it – and after allowing the meat to rest for about 10 minutes, cut into slices about 3 cm thick.

Serve with simple roasted veggies, sweet potato pastries (page 184) and ice-cold, fancy craft beer.

Asian
PORK BELLY
with Banana Dipping Sauce

BY *Petrus Madutlela*

1 deboned free-range pork belly
(check out page 116 to see how
to remove the bone)

coarse salt

FOR THE
MARINADE:

2 stalks lemongrass, crushed

1 litre mirin

150 ml soy sauce

2 cloves garlic, crushed

2 red chillies, finely chopped

50 g fresh ginger, finely
chopped

Once you've deboned the pork belly, get your hands on a really sharp knife and score the skin in a crisscross pattern (each cut should be about 1 cm apart). Generously rub the entire belly with the coarse salt.

Mix all the marinade ingredients together in a large saucepan and bring to the boil.

Place the pork belly in a large roasting tin and pour the hot marinade over the meat. Leave to infuse for 3–4 hours. Remove the pork belly and pat the skin-side dry.

Braai over low coals, meat-side down first. Turn the belly over after about 1 hour and then braai the skin-side for another hour. Be careful of the heat of your coals though – if it's too hot, the meat will burn. Once you've got the perfect crispy crackling, take it off the heat and allow to rest before carving. Serve sliced with a side of the banana dipping sauce.

FOR THE BANANA DIPPING SAUCE:

Mash together 2–3 bananas. Cook them in a fireproof pan over moderate coals, and then add 2 tablespoons of Greek yoghurt and ½ tablespoon of wholegrain mustard.

LÜDE

While most road trips consist of only one or two destinations, ours consisted of 13, and while it's great to have a change of scenery as often as we do, it also involves a lot of planning and logistics. After our river adventures, it was time to pack up yet again and travel deeper into the heart of Namibia. When you road trip with a group of people as large as ours, there are so many things to keep in mind, and the most important is probably considering where everyone will sleep... and what they'll eat. Namibia, for all its big wide open spaces, only has a couple of places that can accommodate a group as large as ours and this was taken into consideration before we even left home, and it's something you should think about too before just hitting the road. Planning your trip properly is *always* a good idea.

Our next destination was a place I'd been to before many years ago and with a busload of great friends. It's the small harbour town of Lüderitz, which is an obscure place and stands in isolation on the frontier of the great dune sea and the rich, cold Benguela current that runs up the west coast of Africa. This area is pretty much as it was when, in 1487, Portuguese navigator Bartolomeu Dias stopped here on his way to find a sea-trade route to spice-rich India. For the next 400 years it remained an obscure anchorage on a barren part of the African coast. But with the discovery of diamonds the area boomed, and the town itself became an enclave for the 'Sperrgebiet' or the forbidden zone – 26 000 square kilometres of coastal desert that is rich in diamonds, thanks in a large part to the Orange River that, because of her reverse current up the coast, leaves a scattering of these precious stones behind. The Sperrgebiet runs all the way from the Orange River in the south

ÜRITZ

into the dune fields of Namibia in the north, stretching to the horizon and beyond. The town itself was founded in 1883 and is famous for its Art Nouveau architecture. It started as a trading post, but for a short period it became the bustling centre of activity during the diamond rush in the early 1900s. Testament to this is the ghost town of Kolmanskop – an old mining town on the outskirts of Lüderitz – and a definite must-see when you're there. My advice? Don't do a guided tour – rather take your time and spend a couple of hours exploring this deserted town that lies at the mercy of the Namib Desert, which is slowly engulfing the once grand buildings.

Travelling to Lüderitz is an adventure in itself and you will soon feel like you are the only person driving on that road. Our suggestion? Follow the Orange River and take the back road, not the tar road. Look for an adventure! I think we drove past five cars in total on our way there – and the journey took over seven hours, so imagine just how isolated you'll feel on that long stretch of road. My only advice: when you're driving on this road, do it slowly – there are loads of animals to spot, including Namibia's wild horses, Gemsbok and Springbok, a wonderful sight to see. Keep your eyes peeled – there are no fences out here and these wild animals cross the road when you least expect it. The landscape also changes dramatically, from incredible rock formations and quiver trees and then, before you know it, you're suddenly surrounded by the most beautiful red dunes. Words can do little justice to describe driving here – I suggest you get in your car and do it yourself.

Wherever we travel to, we try to stick to what the locals eat as much as possible. And Lüderitz is well known for three more things, other than diamonds. Snoek, oysters and crayfish. Even though the crays were out of season, we created a few dishes inspired by this abundance of seafood.

SNOEK

& Patat Soup BY Petrus Madutlela

YOU NEED

1 kg snoek, vlekked (see page 132) and braaied

olive oil

1 onion, chopped

1 clove garlic, crushed

½ chilli, seeded and chopped

1 x 410 g tin chopped tomatoes

a pinch of sugar

salt and pepper to taste

a pinch of saffron

1 punnet of cherry tomatoes

1 litre organic chicken stock

2 sweet potatoes, peeled and cubed

6 pickling onions, peeled

6 bulbs fennel, halved

Once you've braaied your snoek, set it aside to cool. Heat a glug of olive oil in a flat-bottom potjie over moderate coals. Fry the onion, garlic and chilli until fragrant and soft, then add the chopped tomatoes, sugar, salt and pepper, saffron, cherry tomatoes, chicken stock and sweet potatoes, and simmer.

In the meantime, chargrill the whole pickling onions straight on the grid, then take them off the heat. After about 20 minutes, add the fennel and onions to the soup and continue simmering. While that's on the go, the snoek should have cooled down, so flake it into a bowl – but make sure that you remove all the bones. Add the flaked snoek to the simmering soup and continue to cook for about 5 minutes. Ladle the steamy soup into mugs, bowls or whatever other dishes you have handy and serve with crusty bread.

LÜDERITZ

Fig. 45.—Snoek (*Thyrsites atun*).

Kassie

This has become a very popular and versatile little braai friend on the road. The idea is very simple and although it rattles while you travel, it's totally worth making one.

YOU NEED:

1 x 25-litre brand new (and empty) paint drum with lid (obviously not a plastic one...)

1 wire rack that will fit inside the drum

That's it. These two things open up a whole new braai world and the things you can do with it are endless! The bonus? It's small enough to fit in your car, so you can take it anywhere.

SMOKING:

To use the kassie as a smoker, you need three things: the protein, some wood chips and a fire. Simple, right?

BAKING:

The kassie easily turns into a self-contained little oven. When you lay it down sideways, straight on top of the coals, put the wire rack into the centre and whatever you want to bake on top of the rack, and you're good to go.

PIZZA:

You don't need a fancy pizza oven to bake a deliciously cheesy pizza. It's got that same wood-baked taste and you can do it anywhere.

LUDERITZ

⌐ = 5-25μ
⌐ = 1,6-5μ
⌐ = 0,25-1,6μ
⌐ = 0-0,25μ
er 02-N-41

NEAVERA

Smoked Snoek Pâté

Apricot jam, butter and snoek are three things that just belong together. When I came up with a new twist on traditional snoek pâté I was stoked. The idea is to first have a layer of snoek pâté, followed by a layer of apricot jam and lastly the butter. And then to eat it on fresh bread. Genius right? Right.

FOR SMOKING:

fillet of 1 fresh snoek, deboned

about 1 tablespoon of smoking chips (apple or oak), soaked

FOR THE PÂTÉ:

couple of knobs butter, melted

½ onion, finely chopped

1 clove garlic, crushed and chopped

2 tomatoes, skinned and finely chopped

salt and pepper

1 shot of KWV Brandy

1 handful of finely chopped spring onion

½ x 250 g tub of cream cheese

a splash of fresh cream

a couple of tablespoons of apricot jam

BY *Justin Bonello*

The first thing you're going to do is smoke the snoek. If you're lucky, you've figured out how to make a kassie from watching previous episodes, bush kudos to you! If you don't have your very own kassie at home by now, I suggest one of two things. One, either make a kassie or, two, use a good old kettle braai (works just as well, but isn't half as versatile or impressive as the kassie).

TURN YOUR KETTLE BRAAI INTO A SMOKER:

1. Light a fire.

2. Wait for the coals to form (read: drink a cold beer).

3. Kill the fire by putting the lid on and closing the air intakes.

4. Push the coals to either side of the braai and scatter a small handful of pre-soaked smoking chips over them.

5. Put the snoek fillet on top of the braai grid.

6. Open the air intakes and pop the lid back on.

7. Smoke the snoek for about 10 minutes, then set aside.

8. Once cooled, flake the fish and make sure to discard any bones that you might have missed.

First up, melt a knob of butter and sauté the onion and garlic until soft. Add the flaked, smoked snoek, the chopped tomatoes and season to taste. Once warmed through, add a splash of brandy and flambé. Put the snoek mixture into a mixing bowl, and then stir through the spring onion, cream cheese and cream. Have a taste – if it needs more seasoning, add some, then scrape the pâté into ramekins and flatten the surface with the back of a spoon. Spread apricot jam over the top of the pâté – you can decide how thin or thick you want this layer to be. Follow this by pouring melted butter over the whole lot and pop the pâté into the fridge to cool down. Serve as a pre-braai snack with freshly baked bread. Genius, if I don't say so myself. Oh wait, I already did.

African Snoek & EGGS

BY *Bertus Basson*

When Bertus made this quick breakfast for us on the beach at Lüderitz, he promised us that this would be the best scrambled eggs we would ever eat. And boy, he was right. The way he makes scrambled eggs is a bit of an art, and it makes for the creamiest eggs you'll ever eat.

YOU NEED:

juice of 1 lemon

a couple of tablespoons of apricot jam

about 500 g snoek fillet

9 free-range eggs

about ¼ block butter, cubed

1 big handful of cherry tomatoes, halved

1 handful of chives, chopped

salt and pepper

a couple of lemon wedges for serving

1 loaf of ciabatta, sliced and toasted

Mix the lemon juice and apricot jam together in a bowl. Next, place the fillet of snoek onto a braai grid over moderate coals and braai for about 15 minutes while regularly brushing with the lemon and apricot basting sauce. Once cooked through, but not dried out, take the snoek off the heat and set aside.

Crack the eggs into a cold, fireproof, nonstick pan. Scatter the cubed butter over the top, then move the pan onto a grid over moderate coals. Keep whisking until the butter has melted into the egg and it's cooked through, then remove from the heat. You can even take it off a little bit before the eggs are completely cooked through, as the heat from the pan will continue cooking it.

Flake the fish in biggish chunks and put on top of the eggs. Arrange the halved tomatoes around the pan and finish off with a scattering of chopped chives, salt and cracked black pepper. Serve straight out of the pan with a wedge of lemon and toasted ciabatta. Delicious!

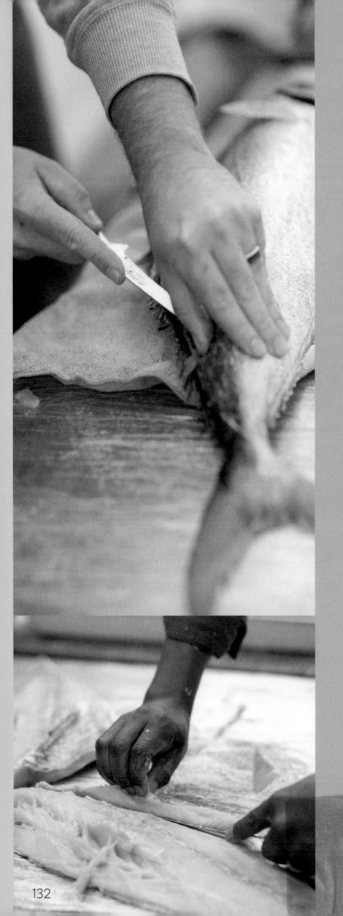

How to VLEK a Snoek

First up, either catch a snoek (good luck) or go get a fresh one from the local fishmonger when the snoek are in season, which is usually in winter. Make sure you vlek the snoek outside – it gets a little messy. Using a sharp knife, cut the snoek open along the backbone, from its tail to its head. Remove the entrails and cut off the head. Wrap the entrails and head in newspaper and keep it to make fish stock (away from any alley cats). Preferably rinse the snoek in salt water (if you're near the ocean) or in cold water (if you're not), then place it, flesh-side up on your working surface. Make an incision down the centre of each fillet – but not so deep that you're cutting through the skin. By doing this you increase the surface area of the snoek. Check for that gang of alley cats, then after generously rubbing salt onto the fish, hang it outside in a cool, windy spot for about 20 minutes to draw moisture out of the fish until it goes tacky. Next, rinse the salt off the fish and pat it dry, before hanging it back in the same spot. Leave it to hang until tacky again.

How to SHUCK Oysters

If you're lucky enough to travel to Lüderitz, you will be able slurp oysters to your heart's content, and for really cheap, which is exactly what we did. But if you don't know how to shuck an oyster you're going to be in trouble... and really disappointed. And a little angry.

Step 1: Get your hands on an oyster-shucking knife. If all else fails you can use a 'flat-point' screwdriver.

Step2: Use a damp dishtowel to hold the oyster firmly while you insert the point of the oyster-shucking knife into the lip/hinge of the oyster.

Step 3: Run the knife from one side of the oyster to the other and, using a twisting motion, push the knife upwards to lift the hinge open.

Step 4: You should now have a perfect oyster sitting in its shell.

Step 5: Give it a quick rinse in sea water to make sure there are no little bits of shell that you could slurp down later – that's not so lekker.

Step 6: Repeat with the abundance of oysters until you've shucked all of them – and keep them on ice until you're going to eat them.

The WORLD is Your Oyster

While we were in Lüderitz we were in oyster heaven. The world literally became our oyster for five beautiful days. Because of how little they cost and how many of them there were, we probably went a little overboard – I imagine it's a little bit like winning the lotto and not knowing what to do with all your sudden wealth. It was a little childish, but absolutely worth it. Here are four of the best oyster recipes from the road, but play around with them and see what you come up with – when it comes to cooking there shouldn't be any real rules.

01

BY *Petrus Madutlela*

Classic Creamy Oysters

YOU NEED:

a big knob of butter

a couple of cloves garlic, crushed

1 cup of fresh cream

white wine

salt and pepper

12 oysters, shucked and removed from their shells

1 small bunch of fresh parsley, chopped

Based on one of the classics, which is usually done with mussels, but this version is equally tasty – good old creamy, garlicky oysters served with fresh bread. And good white wine to wash it down – always.

Melt the butter in a fireproof pan over moderate coals, then add the garlic and fry until fragrant. Add the cream along with a splash of white wine and a pinch of salt and cracked black pepper. Simmer until the sauce is slightly reduced, then add the oysters. Poach them for about 5 minutes, then remove from the heat and stir through the fresh parsley. Serve straight out of the pan with fresh crusty white bread.

MAKE A QUICK SLAW, BY SIMPLY COMBINING:

½ onion, thinly sliced

1 big handful of shredded white cabbage

1 big handful of shredded red cabbage

about 5 radishes, thinly sliced

1 tomato, chopped

mayo (make your own – page 82)

2 chillies, seeded and chopped

YOU NEED:

about 4 oysters per hot dog roll, so count your friends, count the rolls and do the math

½ cup of self-raising flour

1 bottle of beer (any kind)

oil for deep-frying

1 x 250 g packet of streaky bacon

soft, fresh hot dog rolls, sliced

salt and pepper to taste

some lemon juice (optional)

03 The BETTER Oyster Burger

BY *Bertus Basson*

During our five days of gluttony we found a great place that served up oyster burgers. That's right... there are so many oysters that people actually make burgers with them. Imagine! And while it was great, Bertus announced that he could do it better, and so he did.

Once your slaw is done, get the tedious job of shucking the oysters out of the way. Keep them on ice until you're going to cook them. Next, combine the flour and about half of the beer to make a batter – use a wooden spoon and make sure you remove all the lumps.

Heat up a pot of oil over moderate coals, then deep-fry (YES, DEEP-FRY) the bacon until crispy. Remove with a slotted spoon and put on kitchen paper to drain.

Put the oysters into the bowl of batter then, using that same slotted spoon, add them one at a time to the pot of hot oil. Deep-fry until golden and then just as carefully remove them from the oil and place on kitchen paper to drain.

Build your 'better oyster burger' by placing the deep-fried oysters into the sliced buns. Top with strips of crispy bacon and the slaw, season to taste and add a squeeze of lemon juice if you feel like it. Tuck in.

03

BY *Justin Bonello*

BLOODY MARY
Oysters

YOU NEED:

a couple of knobs butter

*a couple of cloves garlic,
crushed*

a shot of vodka

*a couple of tomatoes,
blanched, peeled and chopped*

*2 x 200 ml tins of proper
tomato juice*

*about 12 oysters, shucked and
removed from their shells (but
keep the shells)*

1 stalk celery, finely chopped

Tabasco® sauce

freshly ground black pepper

salt

There are so many set rules when it comes to drink and food, but I like to be creative and change it into something different. Oysters and Bloody Marys are two of my favourite things so, in my mind, combining them makes perfect sense!

Place a fireproof pan over moderate coals, add the butter and once it has melted add the garlic. Fry for a couple of minutes, then add the vodka and flambé. Next, add the chopped tomatoes and the tomato juice and simmer for about 5 minutes. Add the oysters to the simmering juice, along with the celery, poach for 2–3 minutes then take it off the heat. Scoop the oysters back into their shells, add about 1 tablespoon of tomato to each, add a splash of Tabasco, black pepper and a pinch of salt. Slurp them down. If you want, you can add a bit of vodka to each shell too, but that's up to your own taste. I like them without.

SOSSU

We left Lüderitz after having our fill of oysters and snoek and trekked deeper into the desert towards Sossusvlei, situated in the Namib-Naukluft National Park. This is the biggest conservation area in Africa and by size it's the fourth largest park in the world. But at its heart is what is considered to be the most ancient desert in the world – the Namib. This desert's story strangely begins yet again with the powerful Orange River at the heart of southern Africa. For millions of years this river has been grinding her way down to the west coast of southern Africa, depositing massive amounts of sediment into the mighty Atlantic Ocean where the Benguela Current picks it up and carries the sediment along the coast and deposits it on the shore. Here wind picks it up and pushes it inland, forming giant sentinels that have been marching inland for hundreds of thousands of years, eventually forming this great dune sea that is the Namib Desert. But what makes this massive salt and clay pan that is Sossusvlei so incredibly special and rare is that it is surrounded by the world's biggest red sand dunes, including the famous Big Daddy and Dune 45.

USVLEI

Our drive there included the usual off-the-beaten track back roads and on the way we did a detour via Helmeringhausen (yeah... try and say that after a couple of drinks!) to refuel and stock up on supplies before getting back on the road. Driving there, you'll be mesmerised at how the scenery changes every couple of kilometres. After about seven hours and roughly 500 kilometres travelling through some of the most breathtaking scenery, we arrived at the four-star Sossusvlei Lodge. You see, as much as we tough it up out here, every now and then we get treated like royalty, and by this I mean delicious food, warm, comfortable beds and hot showers. We were over the halfway mark and we were tired, so this is exactly what we needed to lift our wilted spirits. This, and a hike to Deadvlei and up the dunes. Trying to describe what Deadvlei (which means 'dead marsh') looks like is difficult. I can tell you you'll feel as if you're walking on Mars, surrounded by the most amazing rusty red dunes. I can tell you that your jaw will drop to the ground in awe. I can describe the blackened camel thorn trees that have been scorched by the unforgiving African sun for almost 900 years. I can tell you that from the top of Big Daddy you'll fully understand the enormity of this ancient desert. Or I can tell you to get in your car and come out here. To hike (and hike, and hike) for what might feel like a very long time (but is actually just 20 minutes). To do it barefoot. And to have a cold beer in your one hand, and a camera in the other. To not be another boring tourist in a safari suit, but to sit there in absolute silence and to experience the power of nature and complete isolation. You'll be so happy you did.

Moon Walking

Have you ever walked on the soft sand of the beach? Cursing at that *one* sand dune that stands in the way of you getting back to your car before your ice cream melts all over your hands? Well, climbing the dunes in Sossusvlei is *nothing* like that. These dunes are different shades of red – the older they are, the redder they are because of the iron oxide rusting them – and they were formed because of sand carried by the wind from the Namibian coast. The sand itself is said to be millions of years old. Millions. Imagine.

But let's talk about walking on these dunes. There are so many to choose from but there are two in my mind that you *have* to climb while you're there, and I suggest doing it during sunset or sunrise. The first is Dune 45, which is only 85 metres high – but high enough for you to enjoy views of the desert in every direction. The second is Big Daddy – and it's exactly that. You will climb, and climb and climb. Your legs will start feeling like jelly and you might start convincing yourself that you're never going to make it to the top. But you will, and at 325 metres the views and horizons that go on into *forever* will make it absolutely worth it. And after climbing and gazing into the sun, the next best thing about these dunes? Running down them without toppling over onto your head and without getting sand in your eyes.

So go on... live a little. I *dare* you.

While some people get annoyed when their car windows get dirty, we embraced it as an opportunity to be 'artsy' – especially when we were stuck next to the road, waiting to film the contestant convoy. And it was always a sad day when one of our car windows got cleaned. But at least we managed to salvage some pictures.

BY *Justin Bonello*

Have you ever tried making your own biltong? Good for you! Have you ever tried making your own biltong in your car while adventuring through the Namibian moonscapes? No? Well... what are you waiting for?

This idea came to me for a couple of reasons. The first is because, obviously, like any true South African, I love biltong. Then there was the thing that we've been desolate for three weeks, travelling through Namibia and I was out of 'tong. But then we arrived at Sossusvlei – renowned for their venison. And art department had some wire. And culinary department had all the spices I needed. And the Sossusvlei Lodge had a huge selection of venison. And so I was game to experiment. And it worked! There is one rule of thumb though – use the best meat you can get your hands on. Cheaper meat is full of sinew and stuff and doesn't make lekker biltong (unless you're making it for a teething baby to suck on).

YOU NEED:

wire – the kind that will bend easily

a car to drive in

a road to take – the longer, the better

venison – I used Kudu; if you're unsure what to use, chat to your butcher (any butcher worth his salt should tell you what the best venison is to use)

tinfoil

Once you've got your meat, cut it into strips – with the grain – about 20 cm long and 3 cm thick. But on this note – if it's hot where you are, cut it thinner – the thicker the cut, the longer it will take to cure and you definitely want to avoid the meat going *vrot*.

When you've cut the meat to its desired thickness and length, it's time to spice it up.

First up you're going to make a dry spice mixture. Mix together equal amounts of:

salt

white pepper

crushed peppercorns

crushed garlic cloves

brown sugar

chilli flakes

To this, add triple the amount of toasted coriander seeds (crushed). Then mix through a couple of pinches of salt – but don't be too heavy handed. There's nothing worse than eating biltong and feeling as if you've just licked an entire salt pan.

When your spice mix is ready, place the strips of meat (one layer) in a glass or stainless steel bowl. Add a sprinkle of spice and then a light drizzle of both Worcestershire sauce and vinegar. Add another layer of meat, more spice and more sauce. Repeat until you've used up all the meat, then cover the bowl and pop it in the fridge for the night.

The next morning before you're about to hit the road, walk to your car with wire, a wire cutter, your car keys, the cured meat and a vague idea of what to do.

First up, and if you're going to do it my way, cover the dashboard with tinfoil to catch the drippings and some of the spices that will inevitably drop off the biltong on the first day. And then it's time to hang it up.

There really can't be any rules here other than don't hang any biltong by an open window (dusty roads), in the boot (too hot), in the engine (too gross), or hovering above your passengers (too rude). What I did was hang it above my windscreen, using my rear-view mirror as an anchor, and getting the wire high enough so that it didn't obscure my view of the road. Make an incision about 2 cm from the top of each piece of meat, thread the wire through the meat, then hang the wire wherever you deem suitable and secure it tightly so that you're free to still go off the beaten track. Get in and travel. This biltong hung in my car for about three days and roughly 1 000 kilometres and by the time we arrived at the Fish River Canyon it was ready to eat. Sadly, with all the crew it only lasted a day but it was worth it – and I would recommend trying this to any bush-cook road tripper out there. Myth. Busted.

149

FISH RIVE

R CANYON

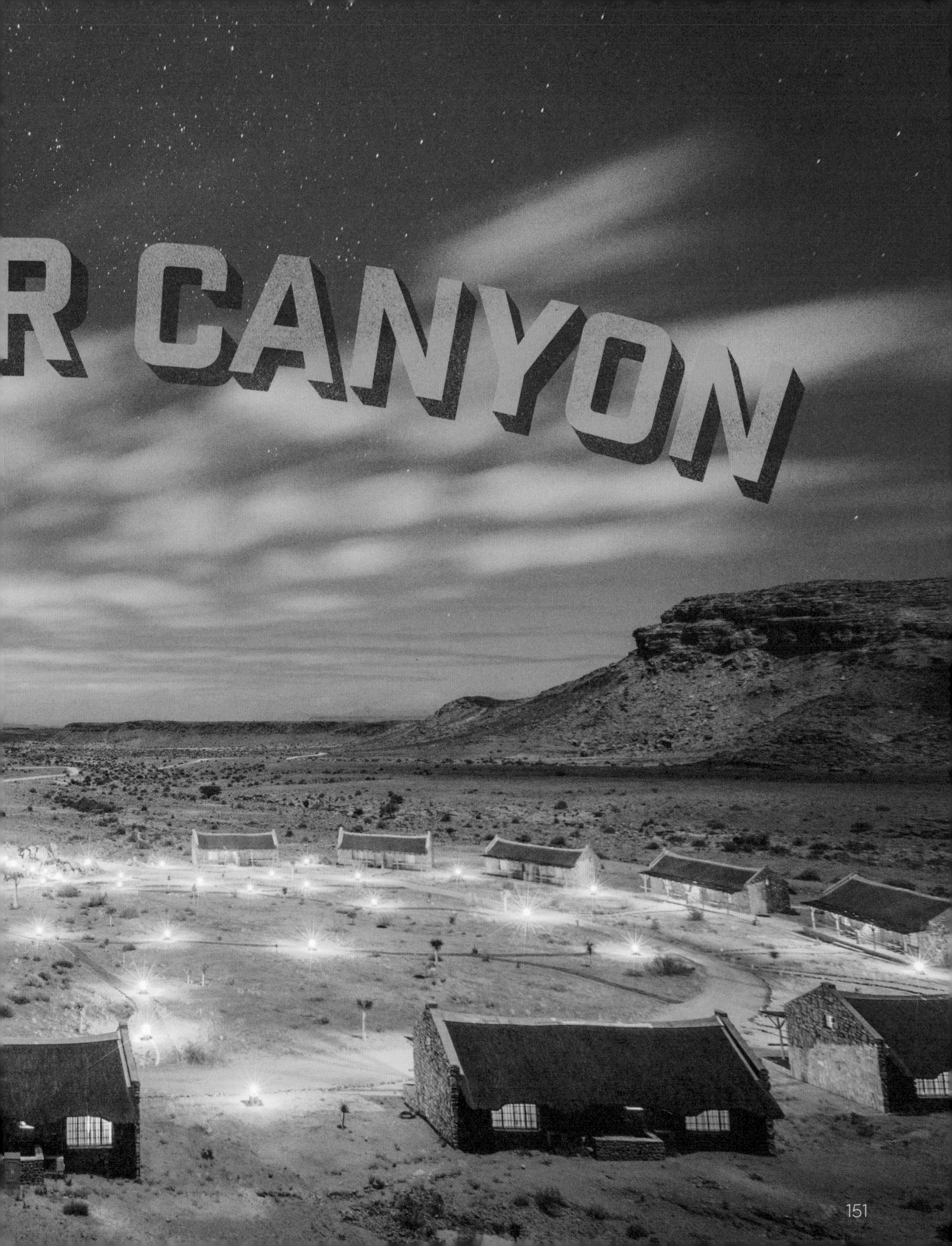

We travelled further south into Namibia to Africa's largest canyon, which is more than 160 kilometres long, 27 kilometres wide and at some places it plunges about 550 metres deep. For goodness' sake, we've got the second largest canyon in the world... you've got to go see it!

The Fish River Canyon started forming more than 600 million years ago – unlike the Colorado that grinds its way through the Grand Canyon all year long, the Fish River only flows seasonally – and it features a system of gigantic gorges, towering rock faces and deep ravines where it can easily reach up to 48 °C in summer and drop almost to freezing on one of those crisp winter nights. The immensity of this landscape is truly breathtaking and you'll be lucky to catch a glimpse of Hartmann's Mountain Zebra, Klipspringer and Chacma Baboon. The most popular activity to do at the Fish River Canyon is to hike it during the right season – but you need to have some tenacity because this 86-kilometre hike is definitely not for the faint at heart. And if you are, try donkey trekking, it will be just as spectacular.

The Fish River Canyon forms another beautiful part of the vast landscapes of Namibia and after being absolutely spoilt by the immensity of the red dunes of Sossusvlei, life just couldn't get any better. While driving to the Canyon Lodge we passed a roadhouse – which is honestly one of the most bizarre things to see in the middle of a desert. And this sparked the idea to have a 'burger and boogie night' the night before we had a day off. After we braaied, we ate and after that we boogied. And there are photos of this night. Scary ones, which involve men in make-up, men dancing with blow-up dolls, friends dancing with friends, bonfires and travelling hippies playing guitar, and just a whole lot of noise. Unfortunately, or maybe fortunately, most of that evening is a blur for the majority of the crew. But it's always a good idea to blow off some steam – especially when the next day is a relaxing one. And while a lot of the crew spent it inside their chalets behind their laptop screens watching series and feeling sorry for themselves, others climbed the hills and sweated out their sins before returning to the bar.

It was one of our most *unforgettable forgettable* stays in Namibia. And one you should definitely experience for yourself (the beauty of the canyon, *not* the raucous party – unless you want to).

Desert Ice Cream

This is not just *any* kind of ice cream. This is the kind of ice cream that you can make when you're in the great outdoors, in the middle of nowhere and even under the hot African sun in the middle of the desert like we were. And if you're at home and you want to make this, go ahead and use a fancy ice-cream machine if you have to. But let me tell you... being able to make your own with only a cooler box, ice and salt to make it work, that's pretty kick-ass!

First up, you're going to make a custard, *AND FOR THIS YOU NEED:*

180 g white sugar

10 free-range egg yolks

500 ml milk

500 ml fresh cream

Whisk together half of the sugar with the egg yolks until creamy and the sugar has dissolved, then set aside. In a saucepan over moderate coals, combine the milk, cream and the other half of the sugar. When it's just about to reach boiling point, remove the milk from the heat then combine with the egg yolk mixture. While the custard is still hot, you're going to whisk in the flavour. This can be anything from cinnamon to vanilla, peanut butter or coffee – add your favourite flavour!

Okay, so now you have lovely hot custard, but how do you turn this into ice cream? Well, it's a fairly easy process, but you do need a bit of patience.

Pour the hot custard into a new vessel (such as a large enamel mixing bowl) and set aside. Fill a cooler box with ice (about halfway), then add about 500 g salt and a couple of splashes of cold water. This drops the temperature of the ice even more – think of it as making a super freezer (also great to do when you have warm beer and little time to wait for it to cool down).

Now nest the enamel bowl into the centre of the box, making sure that the ice covers the sides of the bowl. The more the bowl is in contact with the ice, the faster the ice cream will set. Agitate the mixture regularly by scraping the sides of the bowl where the ice cream slurries are forming. After about 40 minutes your ice cream should be ready! Serve on top of sugar cones or make milkshakes!

Important things to remember:

1. If there's a shady spot, put the cooler box there.

2. Keep the cooler box closed when you're not stirring the custard.

3. Keep stirring the custard – often.

4. Keep scraping the sides of the bowl to get the iced bits.

5. This should take about an hour, max.

6. If it doesn't work, either drink delicious cold custard or try again. But I promise it works... we proved it.

BY *Justin & Bertus*

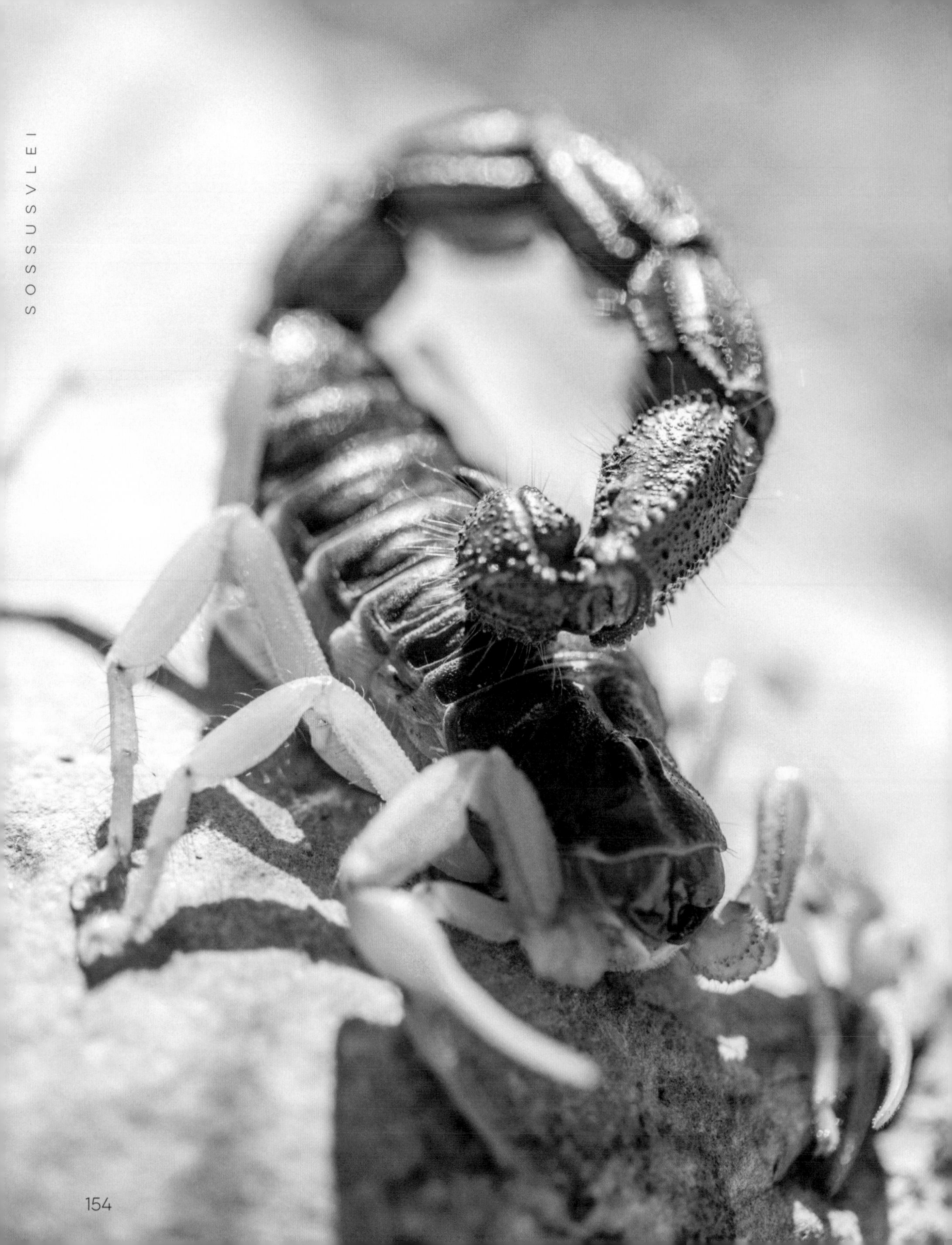

Vegetarian BURGER

- -

For 4 burgers,
YOU NEED:

oil for frying

1 eggplant (brinjal), diced

1 x 410 g tin chickpeas, drained

1 red onion, finely chopped

2 tablespoons of chopped fresh parsley

1 tablespoon of chopped fresh coriander

1 teaspoon of chopped fresh mint

1 teaspoon of ground coriander

1 teaspoon of ground cumin

2 chillies, seeded and finely chopped

2 tablespoons of cake flour

Bertus says that making a vegetarian burger on a braai can be a bit tricky, but his version is like a big falafel made with eggplant. His advice? Fry them in a fireproof pan over moderate coals for your veggie mates (yes, at the same time that you've got the real deal meaty burgers sizzling away on the grid).

First up, heat a splash of oil in a fireproof pan over moderate coals and fry the eggplant until golden brown. Next, place all the remaining ingredients in a mixing bowl, add the fried eggplant, then, using a potato masher, mash all of the ingredients together. Using your hands, shape the mashed veggies and spices into four equal-sized patties and shallow-fry in some oil in a pan over moderate coals.

Serve on a soft roll with your favourite burger garnish.

- -

BY *Bertus Basson*

Parmesan Crusted CHICKEN BURGER

with Fries & a Peanut Butter Milkshake

Hello! Doesn't this just make your mouth water? Doesn't it just make you want to sit in your car at a roadhouse? Windows rolled down, waiting for that perfect fast food mountain to be brought to you while you listen to Elvis Presley on the radio? A burger, fries and milkshake, brought to you by pretty girls with strawberry lips, wearing short skirts. And roller skates. Because it should. Embrace your old school side and make this for your friends. (Short skirts and roller skates optional.)

For 2 ravenous people, YOU NEED:

FOR THE SHAKES:

homemade ice cream (page 153)

4 tablespoons of peanut butter

1 handful of coconut shavings

1 handful of cashew nuts, crushed

FOR THE BURGERS:

2 free-range skinless chicken breasts

about 1 cup of cake flour, seasoned with salt and pepper

2 free-range eggs, whisked

1 cup of grated Parmesan cheese

1 cup of fresh breadcrumbs

1 red pepper

olive oil

1 handful of rocket leaves, chopped

2 cloves garlic, crushed

a few sprigs of fresh mint, chopped

2 hamburger rolls

a few cherry tomatoes, halved

1 head of lettuce, cleaned

1 tomato, sliced

FOR THE FRIES:

4 potatoes

sunflower oil for frying

salt and pepper to taste

The Milkshake...

First up you should get started on the ice cream. It takes some time, and you're making your own. But if you get it right, you'll never want to buy the store-bought variety again. Check out how to make your own ice cream on page 153, adding the peanut butter while the custard is still hot. When your custard reaches double-thick milkshake consistency, simply pour it into milkshake glasses and top with crushed cashew nuts and coconut shavings.

The Burger...

Place the chicken breasts in between two sheets of clingfilm and flatten them by hitting them with a rolling pin (or empty wine bottle, or rock... whichever heavy object you can get your hands on). Coat the breasts in the seasoned flour; dip into the whisked eggs and then coat thoroughly in the grated Parmesan. Dunk them into the egg wash one more time then into breadcrumbs until evenly coated. Set the breasts aside while you get on with the rest.

Take the red pepper and grill it on open coals until the skin is charred and blackened. Remove from the heat and pop it in a ziplock bag to cool and sweat, then remove the skin and core and cut the pepper into segments and coat with a little olive oil. Set aside. Combine the chopped rocket, garlic, mint, a drizzle of olive oil and two big pinches of grated Parmesan and bash it in a mortar and pestle until you have a vibrant green paste.

Heat a glug of olive oil in a fireproof pan and gently fry the chicken patties – about 5 minutes a side until cooked through. Just before the patties are cooked, slice the hamburger rolls in half and toast the insides, then rub the toasted sides with the halved cherry tomatoes. Place some lettuce, grilled pepper, chicken, pesto and a slice of tomato on one half of the bun and top with the other half of the bun.

The Fries:

Simply peel the potatoes and slice them into nice thin sticks. Heat the oil. Fry until golden and crispy. Drain on kitchen paper. Season to taste. PS: If the oil isn't hot enough, you'll end up with oily chips.

BY *Smiler & B.A.*

Justin's Boerewors

I got this recipe from a farmer in the Karoo a couple of years ago, and have since adjusted it and made it my own. So if you ever have the time and patience to make your own boerewors (it's totally worth it) here's one of the best recipes I've ever tried. Give it a shot – even if it's just to try to prove me wrong. Just a word of warning before you start – follow the measurements down to the tee.

YOU NEED:

cleaned sausage casings – you'll be able to get your hands on these at any decent butcher

an electronic scale

a decent mincing machine – anything else will just make this whole effort an absolute nightmare

9.57 kg beef chuck with 34% fat

144 g sea salt

3.3 g white pepper

3.3 g black pepper

3.3 g cayenne pepper

3.3 g crushed cloves

26.6 g ground coriander

4 tablespoons of breadcrumbs

263 ml brown vinegar

10–15 ice cubes

a splash of cold water

First up, put the casings in a bowl of water while you prepare the meat – they're easier to work with when they're moist. Keep the mea cool while you weigh out the spices. Once that's done add the spices to the meat, along with the breadcrumbs, and work it into the meat with your hands. When the meat and spices are properly combined, add the vinegar, the ice and the cold water and stir through the meat again. You're adding the ice simply to ensure that the meat remains cool when you put it through the mincer. Scoop the meat into the top part or 'mouth' of your mincing machine and mince it into a bowl. Quickly heat up a pan, add a splash of oil and fry a small batch of mince. Taste it and adjust the seasoning if necessary but if you're happy with the taste, then it's time to start making boerewors. Next, slip a casing over the funnel and push it back until you only have a tip of the casing hanging off the funnel. Tie the tip into a knot then, holding it, switch the machine on and start pushing the meat through the mincer. Guide the sausage with your hands as the casing fills – be careful not to go too quickly and to not fill the casing up too much otherwise it will burst and then you have to start again. When the casing has been used up, tie the other end into a knot and repeat with fresh casings until you've used up all the meat. Hang the boerewors in a cold room overnight so it can mature slightly and all those lekker flavours can develop. If you don't have the time or the room, just hang the wors in front of a fan or outside in the wind (where the dogs won't get to it) for about 2 hours before braaiing.

Make your favourite boerie rolls – I'm not going to tell you what to do here… every red-blooded South African has their own combinations of what they like. Vacuum-seal and freeze any boerewors that you're not going to eat on the day.

Creature Comforts

JOHN. ART DEPARTMENT. WAIST-BANGLE.
'This was given to me by a sangoma in the Transkei on my first travels years ago. It reminds me of my taste for travelling.'

MISHAL. DATA COWBOY. SKETCHBOOK.
'I always take it with me to hide away in my weird-idea-world when I need to'

DAN. PRODUCTION CO-ORDINATOR. GERMAN BABY BUM CREAM.
'For my lips. Not my bum.'

KIRSTEN. SOCIAL MEDIA GURU. HAIRBRUSH.
'Why should a 70-day, 9000 kilometre road trip stop me from looking gorgeous?'

LUKE. UNIT MANAGER. BEROCCA.
'Do you know what a unit manager does on set? Enough said.'

CARO. FOOD STYLIST. NAIL POLISH. 'Painting my nails reminds me that I am, in fact, female. Especially a good reminder when constantly surrounded by braai smoke and carrying my weight in carrots.'

SIMON. ART DEPARTMENT. BANGLES.
'I've had them forever and in a way they remind me of my mum. That's that.'

MATT. DATA WRANGLER. ROCKS.
'I collect them as a little reminder of all the awesome places we've travelled to.'

SAKI. ART DEPARTMENT. CAP.
'It makes me feel rad. And it's practical.'

JOSH. CULINARY DEPARTMENT. SOCCER BALL.
'I can vent frustration and get exercise at the same time. And it's the easiest way to get a group of people involved socially.'

KAI. CAMERA OPERATOR. CLING CLING.
'The bells were given to me by the Dalai Lama while on shoot with him. I bought the red blood beads in Uganda. The turquoise beads were part of a broken necklace I picked up in the Sinai desert. The African cross was given to me by a Bedouin trader. My cling cling is a talisman I made for my daughter Luna. It was her rattle and she lit up every time she heard the unique noise it makes. I carry it with me EVERY day. I don't get to see her much, so it's my comfort and constant reminder that she loves me.'

ROBBIE. CONTENT DIRECTOR. HACKEY SACK.
'I love my hack because it fits in my pocket and whenever there is time to kill you can play a game. Which is quite often when we pull over to the side of the road.'

BOB. MEDIC. GOOD COFFEE.
'I like to have access to great coffee whenever I want it so I always carry my own.'

MARIONNE. ON-THE-ROAD EDITOR. IPHONE.
'For photos. Music. And long chats with my husband. But most importantly to take photos!'

SUNEL. DIRECTOR OF PHOTOGRAPHY. MAMIYA. 'To snap some personal memories just for me. Also, it's a pretty sexy camera. Who wouldn't want one?'

RAYLENE. EXECUTIVE ASSISTANT. UGGS.
'To keep my feet warm! Cold feet are a big no-no!'

WULA. PRODUCTION ASSISTANT. TIGHTROPE.
'To stay focused & balanced. Helps me switch off from everyday stuff around me.'

LOUIS. PHOTOGRAPHER. POSTCARD.
'It's a postcard of Pablo Picasso which I bought in Paris long ago. It's been travelling with me in my camera bag for the last 15 years. Picasso inspires me.'

SHAUN. CAMERA ASSISTANT BOOK & MUSIC.
'When you're on a two month road trip of epic proportions, the people you travel with undoubtedly become your family... but it's also necessary to have alone time... which is impossible when you are part of a travelling circus, so the best way to escape is with a book and some good music.'

SEAN. PRODUCTION ASSISTANT. LIL'GREEN SKATEBOARD. 'I skate a lot in Cape Town, so every chance I got I was on it because it just felt right. Felt like home.'

Tastes Like Home

Marionne and Helena decided to make their favourite food about halfway through our trip and if you've ever been on the road for the duration that we were, you'll know that this is around the time where you start missing some of the things from home. This longing doesn't last long – usually no longer than a day – and the thing you miss often involves food that reminds you of home. That, and your own bed. And while these two recipes might seem incredibly simple, know that it made two people and a couple of crew members very happy for an afternoon. Also, I wouldn't put these two dishes on the same plate... but they did, and that's okay too.

SMASHED BRITTLE
Salad BY *Marionne Fourie*

YOU NEED:

about 1 cup of sugar

a splash of warm water

a couple of bigs knobs of butter

1 cup of roasted and salted flaked almonds

a couple of handfuls of rocket and baby spinach

about 4 beetroot, peeled and julienned

about 1½ cups of feta, cubed

1 cucumber, cubed

2 avocados, sliced

olive oil

balsamic glaze

salt and pepper to taste

The hardest part of this recipe is making the brittle (yep, it's going in the salad and it's delicious!). Start by making a fire then, once you have moderate coals, place a nonstick, fireproof pan over the heat. Pour in the sugar and a splash of water (just enough to cover the sugar) and let it melt. Once the sugar has dissolved, add the butter and keep stirring. Add the almonds and once you have a lovely golden brown caramel, take the pan off the heat and scrape the brittle out onto a sheet of wax paper.

While the brittle is cooling down, combine all the salad ingredients in a large bowl. Grab a rolling pin (or cover a brick in plastic) and smash the brittle to smithereens. Scatter over the salad, add a drizzle of olive oil and balsamic glaze, season to taste and serve.

PYJAMA PANTS PASTA

olive oil

1 x 250 g packet of streaky bacon, chopped

1 x 250 g punnet of mushrooms – your favourite kind, sliced

a couple of cloves garlic, crushed

a couple of chillies, seeds removed and chopped

1 bunch of spring onions, sliced

a decent splash of dry white wine

salt and cracked black pepper

1 cup of fresh cream

about 5 sprigs of fresh thyme

juice of ½ lemon

your favourite pasta

loads of grated Parmesan cheese

1 handful of fresh basil, torn

This is Helena's go-to pasta when she's looking for that perfect bowl of warm food after a long day, and the best part is that it's really quick to make – even on a fire. She's not going to use this recipe to meet a farmer and marry him, but rather as that guilty comfort food she eats by herself, in bed, where no one can see her.

Once you've chopped and grated and prepped all your ingredients, bring a large pot of salted water to the boil. In the meantime, add a glug of olive oil to a fireproof pan and once hot, add the chopped bacon. Fry for about 5 minutes, then add the mushrooms, garlic, chillies and spring onions and cook for another 5–10 minutes. Add the white wine, salt and pepper and simmer for 5 minutes. Add the cream, fresh thyme and a squeeze of lemon juice and simmer until the cream starts reducing.

By now the water for your pasta should be ready, so add the pasta and cook until al dente. Remove from the heat, drain the excess water and stir through some olive oil. Combine with the sauce and plate up. Serve with loads of grated Parmesan, fresh basil, black pepper and, of course, as Helena would say, only really good dry white wine.

BY *Helena Lombard*

TANKWA

KAROO

Our next destination after enjoying the vast landscapes and silence of Namibia was, well, the vast landscapes and silence of the Karoo. This 400 000 square kilometre semi-desert engulfs a third of southern Africa's landmass. It's a harsh environment where water has always been a scarce commodity and life has had to adapt accordingly – and this is especially true in the Tankwa region. We were headed for the Tankwa Tented Camp, home to the annual AfrikaBurn – the scene of an otherworldly, eclectic and eccentric gathering – and for the next five nights we had it all to ourselves. The Tankwa Tented Camp is situated on a dirt road between Ceres and Calvinia – pretty much in the middle of nowhere. I have a very deep love affair with the Karoo and many South Africans make the giant mistake of just racing past it. Over the last couple of years my crew and I have spent a lot of time out here, and I can tell you that the millions of hectares and blue horizons are a magical place to explore – even during its harshest, ugliest and driest seasons – and for me, especially then. It's difficult to describe this landscape and you'll definitely never fully comprehend why we love it so much unless you actually come here, kick up some dust and explore it for yourself. And while you're out here, make sure you sit around the fire at night and gaze up at the gazillions of stars – they're so bright that you'd be forgiven for thinking that someone slipped something extra into your brandy and coke while you weren't looking.

AfrikaBurn... kind of

While we were in the Karoo, I had *another* birthday on the road – and this one is one I will not easily forget. I say *another* birthday because I can't actually remember the last time I got to be home with my wife and kids and my out-of-office friends. But, as always, my second family were there and we had a great party – AfrikaBurn style. The real AfrikaBurn happens in April every year, and it comes with 20 000 people, a survival guide and a warning that it's not for sissies. Ours was similar. Minus 19 900 people. But judging by the zombie-like state of the crew the morning after, we might as well have been part of the real thing. What lay ahead of us was what would become known as the longest and hottest day in *Ultimate Braai Master* history.

Now, should the travel bug bite you, say around April, and you happen to happen across an event called AfrikaBurn, here are a few things to help you not be *that idiot*:

1. AfrikaBurn is an annual Burning Man regional event.

2. Apparently you don't attend AfrikaBurn... you *create* it.

3. Don't be messy! Make sure you take all your trash home with you and leave the space exactly as you found it.

4. Pack your common sense. People will like you more when you've come prepared for life in the desert.

5. You can't buy or sell anything in Tankwa Town. It's the good old barter system: 'Yo boet, that biltong looks delicious! Can I give you a Bloody Mary for a stick of biltong?'

6. Don't pack your pooch or kitty cat or gold fish. No pets are allowed. Except for guide dogs. Those are cool.

7. Remember your ticket. And ID. And don't hide anyone in the boot of your car. They check. And then you'll have to drive all the way home.

8. Be weather smart. It gets hot as hell during the day and freezing cold at night. So pack appropriately.

9. Have a couple of puncture repair kits or spare tyres in your car. The dirt road to the camp is infamous for eating tyres and spitting them out. The farmers are known to make a roaring profit by selling second-hand tyres to those who are stuck next to the road.

10. Arrive early for the best spot to set up camp.

11. Clean up after yourself. Surely your mother taught you how to do this?

12. If you're in a designated Loud Zone, go ahead and make some noise. If you're in a Quiet Zone, well, shut up. If you want to play music, best set up your camp in the loud zone and if you like your sleep, you know where to go.

13. Always carry water with you. And drink lots of it. Dehydration is not a fun experience.

14. Be prepared for dust storms in whichever way you see fit.

15. Beware the creepies and the crawlies. You're in the Karoo, and this comes with snakes, spiders and scorpions. On that note, remember a first-aid kit.

16. Don't be k*k.

17. If you do *have* to drag your kids along, look after them. Or pay a nanny to do that. Also, try to not lose them.

18. Take a bicycle – it's a necessity and will make getting around Tankwa Town so much easier. Decorate your bike and mark it with your name, phone number and area you are camping at. Also, lock it, but obviously not when you're cruising on it.

173

LAAAMB!

If you're an old (dusty) shoe in the Karoo you'll know that it's home to a unique and hardy breed of sheep farmers, and so it made sense for us to pay homage to the sheep – and while the contestants who were still on the road trip had to make an array of lamb dishes, from snout to tail, we had time to kill and decided to make our own little fuss-free lamb braai on the side.

Lamb Kofta

YOU NEED:

400 g minced lamb

2 heaped teaspoons of chopped fresh coriander

1 heaped teaspoon of coriander seeds, toasted and crushed

1 heaped teaspoon of cumin seeds, toasted and crushed

2 cloves garlic, chopped

1 tablespoon of smoked paprika

1 teaspoon of cayenne pepper

loads of salt and pepper

metal skewers

Great pre-braai snack... or add some pita bread and tzatziki for a great lunch!

Mix all of the ingredients together in a large mixing bowl, and knead the mince thoroughly until properly combined. Shape into balls and fit three on each skewer. Place on a braai grid over moderate coals and braai, turning them often until browned on all sides. You want the koftas to be juicy, so make sure you don't overcook them.

While the koftas are on the go, lightly toast some pita breads and make a little salad by mixing together thinly sliced cucumber, chopped red onion and mint.

BY *Bertus Basson*

BY *Bertus Basson*

Lamb FLATTY

For 6 friends, *YOU NEED:*

*1 leg of lamb, deboned
(see page 179)*

3 cups of Greek yoghurt

1 teaspoon of cayenne pepper

1 tablespoon of paprika

1 tablespoon of ground cumin

1 tablespoon of fennel seeds

*2 tablespoons of chopped
ginger*

4 teaspoons of chopped garlic

1 tablespoon of chopped chilli

4 tablespoons of brown sugar

salt to taste

juice of 2 limes

Deboned leg of lamb. Marinated in a spicy yoghurt sauce. Braaied over perfect coals. Sliced and served straight off a wooden board. Enough said.

Once you've deboned the lamb, mix the remaining ingredients together, then place the lamb in a large roasting tin, marinade and pop it in the fridge and leave overnight.

The next day, and once your coals are at a moderate heat, place the meat in a sandwich grid and braai slowly, continuously basting with the leftover marinade. The lamb should be perfectly caramelised on the outside and pink (but not raw) on the inside. If you like yours more cooked than that (sacrilege!), braai it for longer.

Rest the meat for about 10 minutes before carving, then sprinkle over a pinch of coarse salt and fennel seeds, and add a last squeeze of lime to freshen up the dish and cut through some of the fattiness of the meat.

Lamb

BY *Louis Hienstra*

SOSATIES

YOU NEED:

cubed leg of lamb (to see how to debone one, check out page 179)

a small handful of crushed garlic

salt and pepper to taste

the juice of 1 lemon and an extra 1 to use when you braai

a splash of olive oil

a small hand of rosemary

red onion, quartered, to go on the skewer

metal skewers

It's easy to buy those ready-made sosaties at the shops, but why do that when you know you can do it better? Exactly. My photographer took a few hours downtime while shooting the 24-hour challenge to make these. They're pretty tasty. Serve these with pap, relish and salad. Good old braaivleis at it's best.

After you've cubed the leg of lamb, pop the meat along with all the marinade ingredients into a large mixing bowl. Let it rest in the marinade for at least 1 hour, then thread the cubed meat and a quartered red onion onto the skewers until you've used up all the meat.

Braai the sosaties over moderate to hot coals for about 20 minutes, turning them often and basting with the leftover marinade as you go. Squeeze some extra lemon over them just before they're done. Serve seasoned with salt and pepper.

How To
DEBONE
a Leg of Lamb

When you debone a leg of lamb, it cuts down the cooking time from 1–2 hours to about 45 minutes, it won't be raw on the bone as it sometimes can get and you still have all that lekker fat that lubricates the meat, keeping it moist and juicy while it's cooking.

1. Start by making an incision down the big main bone, lengthways, and then do the same on the other side.

2. Carefully remove the meat on the one side by repeatedly cutting the meat as close to the bone as you can. You'll notice that the more you keep repeating this, the more the bone will become visible, which is what you want.

3. As soon as the bone is loose from the sides and fully exposed, start cutting underneath it to free it from the bottom.

4. Cut off the bone and the shank - you can use the shank for a stew later.

5. Cut off any cartilage and big lumps of fat inside the meat.

6. Now it's time to butterfly the lamb, to ensure that the meat will cook evenly.

7. Look for where the biggest chunk of meat is (usually at the top side of the leg) and cut it open by slicing it in half, but be careful not to cut straight through it. Imagine opening up a book in the middle – that's the kind of incision you're going to make.

8. Next, make a few incisions into the middle part of the lamb so that it's roughly the same height as the meat you just cut. Do the same with the last section of the meat.

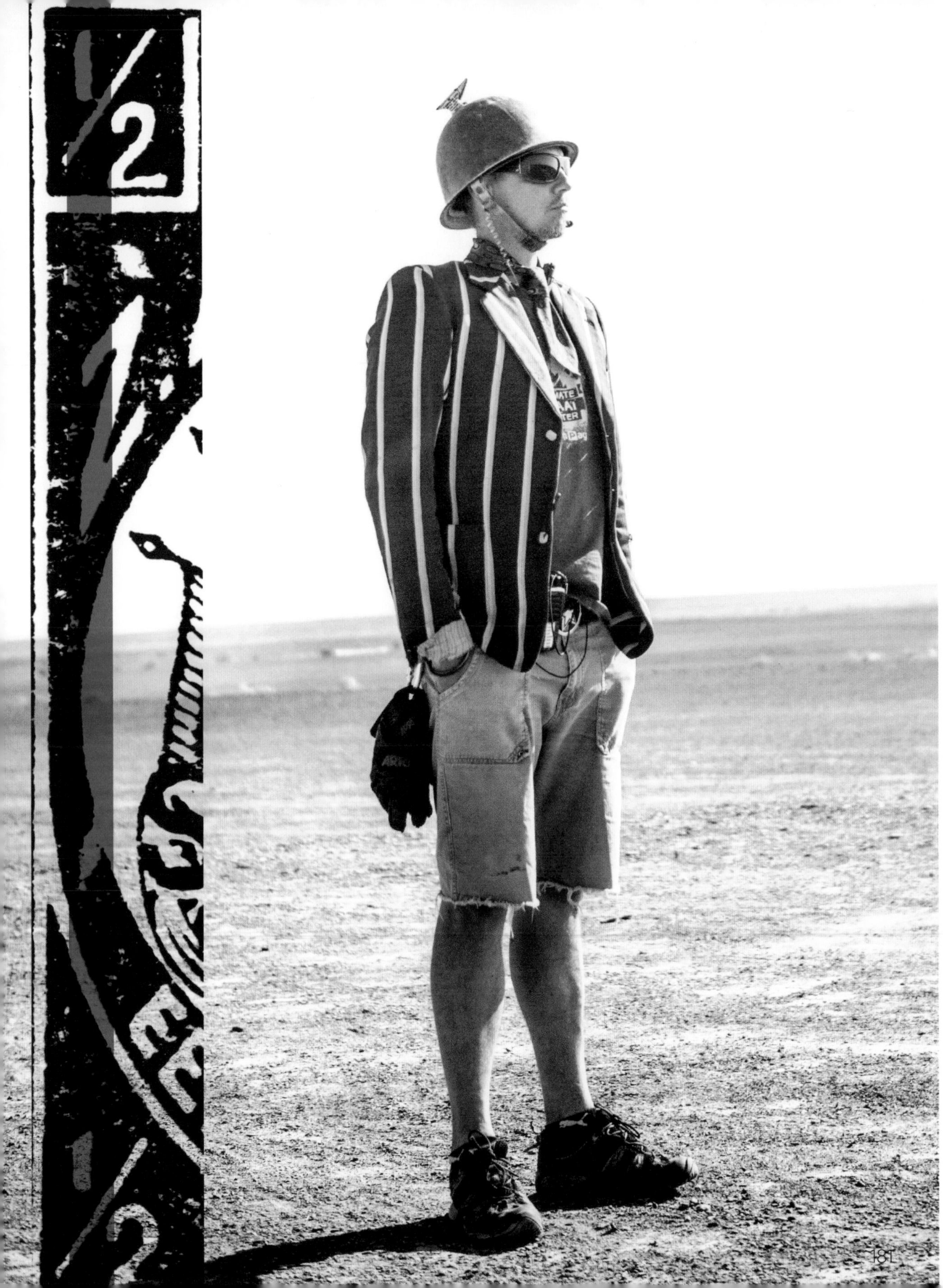

All About Pap

Petrus claimed the title of Ultimate Pap Master on the road, and with good reason. He just *knows* how. And if you're a bit of a pap novice (or always scratching your head as to why your pap never comes out as you would like it to – think burnt at the bottom, still raw, or lumpy instead of crumbly) – then here are four different varieties for you to practise – and get right the first time.

SOFT PAP

4 cups of water

2 teaspoons of salt

1 cup of maize meal

2 tablespoons of butter

Boil the water over moderate coals, then add the salt. Scrape away some coals to reduce the heat, then stir in the maize meal, pouring it in in a slow, steady stream – if you want to, use a whisk to make sure that the pap is nice and smooth. Cover the potjie and simmer over a low heat for about 30 minutes, stirring occasionally and adding more water if required. Once cooked, stir through the butter and serve.

FERMENTED PAP

Step 1. Fermentation:

4 cups of water

3 cups of maize meal

Combine the 4 cups of water and maize meal and leave to ferment somewhere overnight – in a warm area between 25 and 30 °C. The next day, you'll notice the pap mixture smells sour and yeasty.

Step 2. Cooking:

2 cups of water

2 teaspoons of salt

2 tablespoons of butter

Bring the 2 cups of water to the boil over moderate coals, then add the salt and the fermented pap, stirring well until properly combined. Simmer for 25–30 minutes or until cooked, then stir the butter into the pap just before serving.

KRUMMELPAP

3 cups of water

2 teaspoons of salt

4 cups of maize meal

2 tablespoons of butter

Bring the water to the boil over moderate coals, then add the salt and maize meal. Reduce the heat of the coals, cover the potjie and simmer for 10 minutes. You'll notice a skin has formed on the surface – when this happens, take a fork and work it through the pap until it crumbles. Cover the potjie again and simmer for 30 minutes over a low heat until cooked, soft and crumbly. Stir the butter through just before serving.

STYWEPAP

4 cups of water

2 teaspoons of salt

2½ cups of maize meal

2 tablespoons of butter

Pour the water into a flat-bottom potjie and bring to the boil over moderate coals. Add the salt and then the maize meal so that it forms a pyramid in the centre, but don't stir it. Reduce the heat of the coals by scraping a few to the side, pop the lid on and simmer for about 10 minutes. Remove the lid and, using a wooden spoon, stir the maize meal into the water, working it until it's lump free. Pop the lid back on again and simmer the pap for 25–30 minutes. Stir the butter into the pap just before serving.

BY *Petrus Madutlela*

Sweet Potato
ROLY POLY

This recipe belongs to Maryke, who was stuck in the kitchen tirelessly making food for the 70 modern nomads – we ate some of the best food of the trip out here in the middle of nowhere – but then again, that's what the Karoo is so famous for: the hospitality and the great food.

One night, she made these pastries as a side to the snoek braai the guys were doing for us, and it went down a real treat! Although she didn't do it on the fire, this recipe *has* to be shared. But if you want to make it on the braai, go ahead and do that – just use a flat-bottom potjie and make sure the coals aren't too hot.

She's made this recipe for years and years, and can probably do it with her eyes closed by now.

1.5 kg sweet potatoes, peeled and cut into 5-mm-thick slices

2 knobs of butter

1 cup of brown sugar

4 cinnamon sticks

a pinch of salt

phyllo pastry

1 cup of fresh cream

2 tablespoons of brown sugar

BY Maryke

This is how you do it (but keep your eyes open):

Layer the sweet potato slices, butter and brown sugar in a heavy-bottom pot, add the cinnamon sticks and salt, then cook it very gently until the sweet potato is soft. Take it off the heat and let it cool down slightly.

In the meantime, layer two sheets of phyllo pastry on a clean surface. Remove the cinnamon from the pot and set it aside. Roughly mash the sweet potato, then scoop a thick row of sweet potato on top of the pastry and roll it up. Cut the roll into 4-cm-thick slices and arrange in a greased baking dish – in the same way you would a traditional roly-poly pudding. Keep repeating the pastry rolling and cutting until you've used up all the sweet potato. Take the cinnamon sticks that you put aside earlier and arrange them in between the rolls of pastries. Mix together the cream and 2 tablespoons of brown sugar and pour it over the top. Pop the baking dish into a preheated oven (180 °C) and bake for 30–40 minutes or until golden brown.

Serve with fish, meat or chicken. It'll soon become a crowd favourite amongst your friends.

BY *Tippie & Santie*

White
CHOCOLATE
Baked Cheesecake

For one delicious cheesecake, *YOU NEED:*

1 x 250 g tub cream cheese

4 tablespoons of fresh cream

½ cup of castor sugar

1 free-range egg

about ⅓ of a normal slab of white chocolate

½ packet Nutty Crust ™ cookies, crushed

2 tablespoons of butter

your favourite fresh berries

If you thought the only place you could bake a cheesecake is in the comfort and warmth of your kitchen, while sipping tea and paging through glossy magazines while you wait for the cake to bake, you are wrong. This is definitely a sweet treat for the ladies to make and enjoy... around the fire. And it's easy enough for a man to do it too.

In a large bowl, mix together the cream cheese and fresh cream and half the castor sugar, then add the egg and combine well. Heat a pot of water over hot coals, then balance a glass bowl over the simmering water. Break the chocolate into the glass bowl and melt, then stir it into the cream cheese and egg mixture and set the filling aside. Next, take the crushed cookies and mix them with the butter until it becomes sticky, then press the mixture into a round baking tray. Pour the cheesecake filling over the crust – to about the three-quarter mark. Place the tray into a bigger flat-bottom potjie and place the potjie over very low coals. Pop the lid on, scatter a few coals on top of the lid and bake for 25–30 minutes. Check if the cake is ready after 20 minutes – you'll know it's done when it's light brown in colour and starting to crack a little. Remove from the heat and set aside to cool. Mix the berries with the rest of the sugar and use them to decorate the top of the cheesecake. Dust with icing sugar... and voila! A delicious braaied cheesecake!

OUDTS

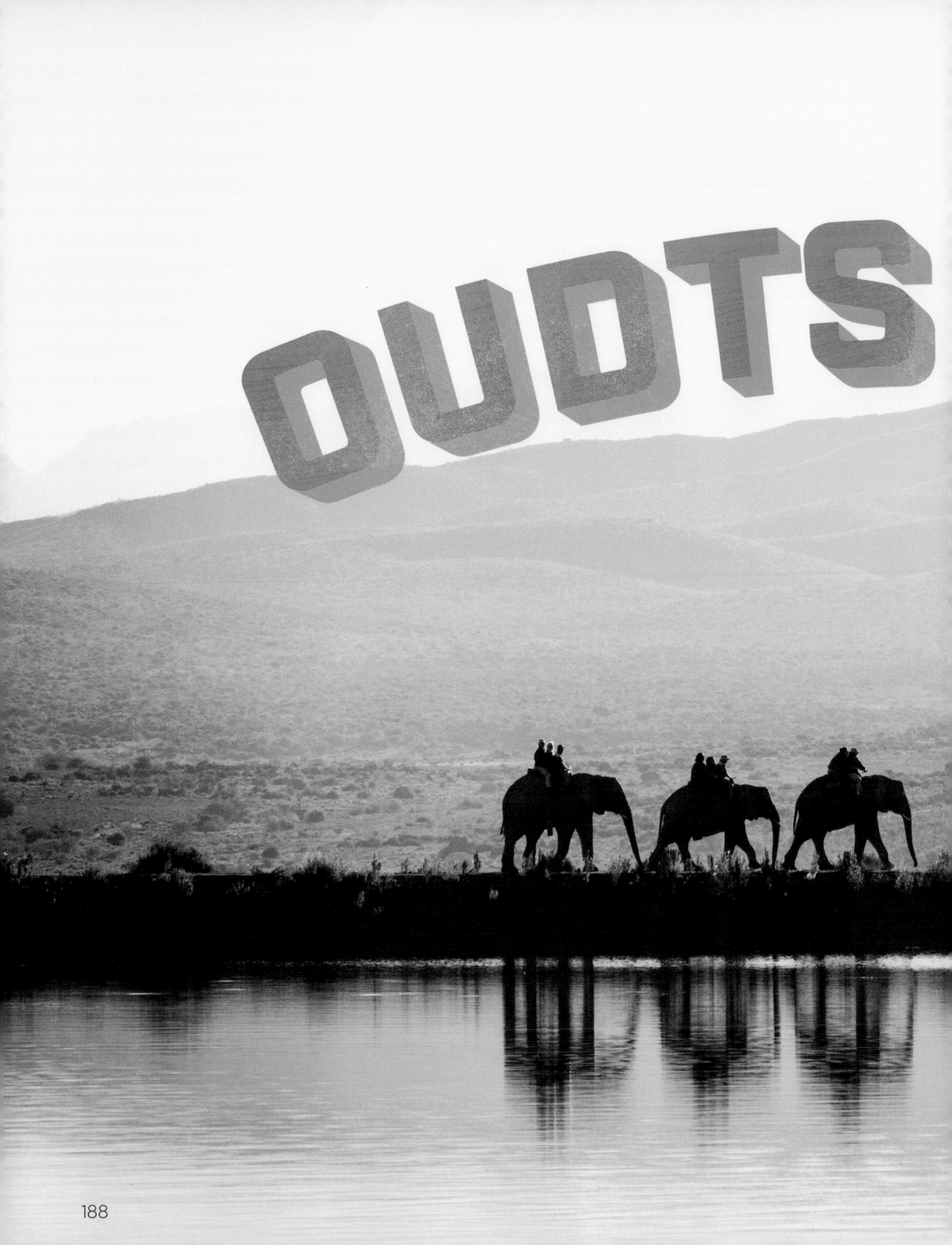

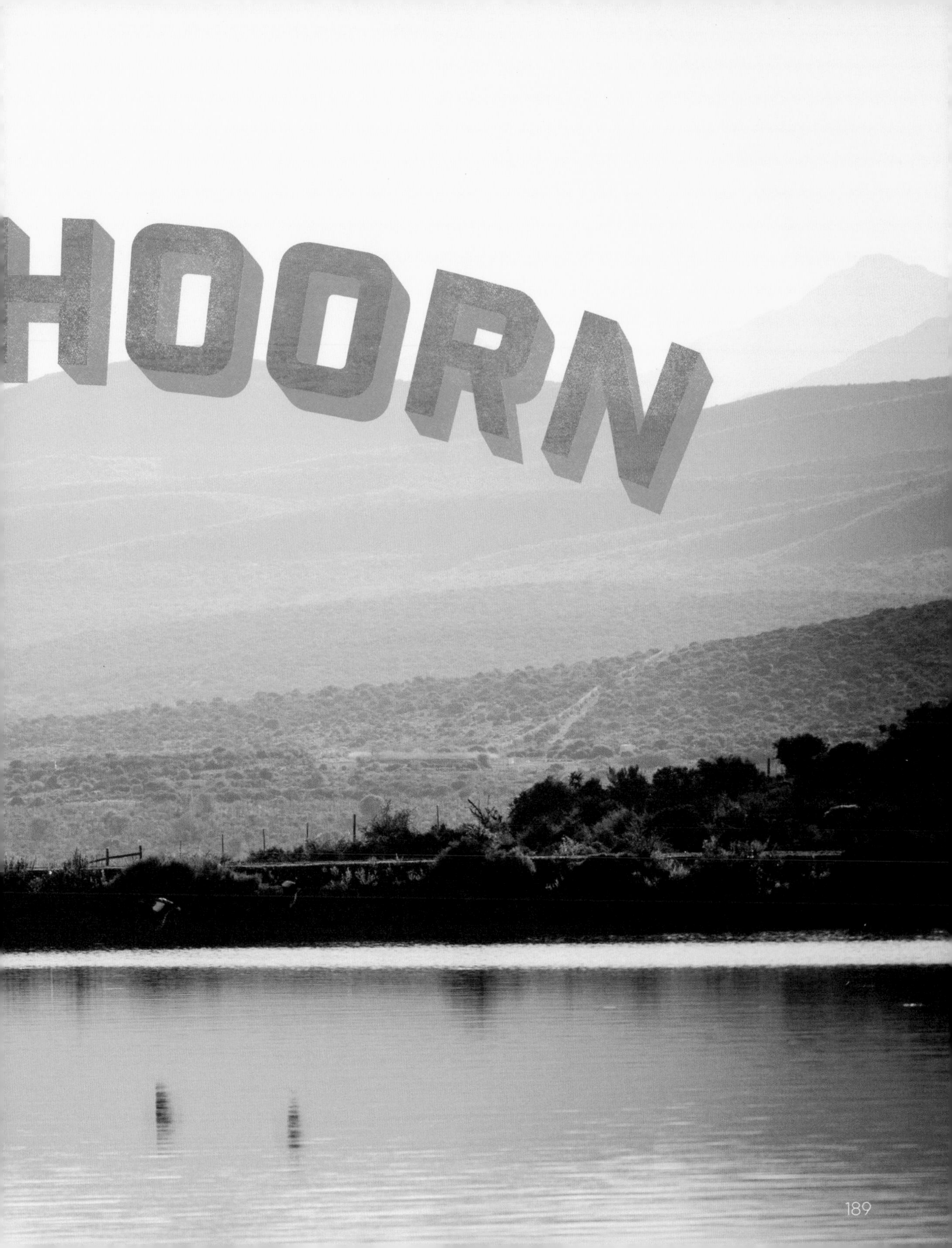
HOORN

Time for CHILL!

Yes, okay, so even though this year's show's official season title was 'Time for Tough' we were nearing the end of our two-month, 9 000-kilometre road trip. And we were tired. Dog tired. As tired as worn-out shoes. And ready to head back home. In fact, we were only 500 kilometres away from the Mother City, which after travelling for nearly 9 000 kilometres felt like it was literally just around the corner. The Buffelsdrift Game Lodge was our second-to-last destination and, after roughing it in the Tankwa Karoo, we were happy to rest our weary heads on big puffy pillows, to sleep under feathery duvets and to eat five-star cuisine – this is the stuff you dream of when you're on the road. We might be a travelling circus, but we're still human. Adventurous humans, who knew that the Swartberg Pass was nearby and, of course, we never miss out on an opportunity to stretch our legs somewhere where there are views in every direction. This is probably South Africa's most famous pass – it separates the Great Karoo from the Little one – and, at about 1 500 metres above sea level, overlooks the ostrich capital of the world: Oudtshoorn. This small Karoo town's fortune was built around the ostrich boom on the insatiable demand for feathers. So, if you're ever in the area, spend some time at the Buffelsdrift Game Lodge for some serious R and R. And take a drive on the Swartberg Pass. It's so worth it. And then tuck into some ostrich steaks... after all, local is lekker!

BREAKFAST

Do you know how you can tell that you're finally relaxing on a road trip? When you get to sleep in. When you start getting a sunglasses tan. When you fall asleep at eight at night, thinking it's after midnight already. When you spend more time reading than you do actually having conversations with people. When you forget what day of the week it is and when you stop looking at your watch. All of that and then when you have time to actually plan and cook an impressive breakfast. Or three.

Smoked Trout & Quail Eggs

BY *Yusuf & Stephen*

YOU NEED:

1 trout fillet, cut into four equal pieces

1 small handful of gooseberries

about ½ cucumber, thinly sliced

1 avocado, peeled and sliced

1 small handful of fresh dill

your favourite micro-herbs

juice of ½ lemon

olive oil for drizzling and frying

salt and pepper to taste

4 quail eggs

1 passion fruit

2 big dollops of crème fraîche

First up, fillet and debone the trout and place it on a wire rack (one that will fit into an oven tray). Scatter a small handful of smoking chips at the bottom of the tray, place the rack and trout over it, then cover the whole lot with tinfoil. Place on a grid over medium to hot coals to smoke and cook the fish (10 minutes should do the trick).

While the fish is smoking, put together a salad using the gooseberries, cucumber, avocado and herbs and finish it off with a squeeze of lemon and a drizzle of olive oil.

By now your fish should be done, so remove it from the smoker and let it cool slightly. Remove the skin, then pop it in a pan with a dash of oil, salt and pepper and fry until crispy. While that's on the go, heat another pan over moderate coals. Add a splash of oil then fry the quail eggs, sunny-side up. Scoop out the passion fruit's pulp and mix with the crème fraiche, then season to taste. At this point, the eggs should be ready and the skins should be crispy. Remove from the heat and set aside. Arrange everything in two bowls, any which way you want, and serve with an extra squeeze of lemon, salt and pepper.

Hot Smoked Trout
with Rösti, Poached Eggs & Velouté

FOR THE KICK ASS SMOKED TROUT:

2 trout fillets, cleaned and deboned – keep the bones

1 small handful of sugar

1 small handful of salt

1 kassie (check it out on page 126)

1 cup of wet woodchips

VELOUTÉ:

the bones of the trout you deboned and set aside

½ cup of dry white wine

1 tablespoon of dried chilli flakes

1 bay leaf

2 tablespoons of butter

2 tablespoons of cake flour

POTATO ROSTI

1 medium potato, peeled and grated

1 free-range egg, whisked

1 small handful of cake flour

olive oil for frying

salt and pepper to taste

(This pretty much translates into: Kick-ass fish and eggs with some awesome sauce and potato cakes)

First up, rub salt and sugar into the trout and set aside. Get the kassie on the fire and, as soon as it's very hot, put the woodchips inside. Once the chips start smoking, place the trout fillets on top of the grid, pop the lid on and smoke them for a maximum of 15 minutes.

While the fillets are being smoked, start making that awesome sauce.

Put the bones, wine, chilli and bay leaf into a potjie over moderate coals, and then cover with water. Simmer gently for about 30 minutes, then strain the stock and make sure you've removed all the bones.

Next take a pan, melt the butter and whisk the flour into the butter to make a roux. Once done, add your fish stock a little bit at a time, whisking continuously to prevent it from going lumpy. As soon as the sauce starts to thicken, simmer it gently for about 5 minutes, then take it off the heat.

Squeeze any excess moisture out of the grated potato then put the potato in a mixing bowl. Add the egg and flour, season to taste and mix into the grated potato until it forms something resembling a stiff batter.

Heat some olive oil in a pan over hot coals and then scoop spoonfuls of rösti batter into the hot oil. Shallow-fry until cooked through and golden brown on both sides.

So your sauce is ready, the potato röstis are perfect and the fish is beautifully smoked. The last thing you have to do is poach some eggs and you're done.

Put the fish on top of a rösti, top with a poached egg and a generous drizzle of sauce. Serve with champagne… just because you can.

BY *Tippie & Santie*

Ostrich Egg

Did you know that one ostrich egg is equivalent to 24 chicken eggs? That can feed a whole lot of people. I've always wanted to try this but didn't have the time to. Lucky for you, Caro (Food Stylist), Petrus and Saki (Props Master) had some time to kill and they gave it a shot.

Step one:

Hold the egg firmly in one hand. If you drop it on your foot, either the egg or your foot might break – I can't be sure which one. If you want to, place a large napkin into a bowl big enough to fit the egg into. So imagine the egg being nestled inside the napkin.

Step two:

Take a sharp, heavy-ish knife, concentrate on where you put your fingers and perforate a line around the top part of the egg, by lightly tapping around the egg.

Step three:

This is where it might start to get a little tricky. Open the egg up along the line that you made with your knife. Do this by peeling it off in bits.

Step four:

Carefully pour the contents of the egg into the bowl – the trick is to keep the yolk intact by making sure it doesn't pop, so make sure that the hole you just made in your egg doesn't have any sharp edges.

Step five:

Heat a large, fireproof pan over moderate coals and add a decent glug of olive oil and a large knob of butter.

Step six:

Once the butter has melted and the oil is hot, carefully pour the egg into the pan. Fry until it's done to your liking.

Serve straight out of the pan, unless you can figure out how to get it out without breaking the whole thing. My suggestion? Season with salt and pepper, hand out some forks and toast and let your friends eat it straight out of the pan.

Warning: Ostrich egg is an acquired taste!

de Grandeur Naturelle

THREE STEAK CLASSICS
with an Ostrich Twist!

We had to. We were in the Ostrich Capital. I'm not the biggest fan of ostrich meat, but a lot of you are, so I've included it. If you don't like ostrich either, just replace it with beef fillet. Admittedly, I've given you these recipes in previous books, but it's always good to include old favourites. And they are classics for a reason, and I don't know who has any of my other books and who doesn't. If you don't... bastard, but thanks for buying this one! If you have the copy of my book with these three recipes, then feel free to write to me and k*k me out.

Anyway, let's get on with it.

Carpetbagger

YOU NEED:

4 ostrich fillet steaks

12 fresh oysters, shucked

about 2 teaspoons of crumbled mild blue cheese

about 2 teaspoons of chopped fresh parsley, plus extra to garnish

4 teaspoons of dried breadcrumbs

butter, at room temperature

salt and cracked black pepper

olive oil

BY *Penny & Dee*

Old school makes a comeback! And it's still as delicious as it was back in the 80s...

First up, make an incision into the side of each ostrich fillet to create a pocket for the stuffing. After you've shucked the oysters (check out page 133 to see how), lightly smoke them in a kassie (and to see what a kassie is and how to use it as a smoker go to page 126). After you've smoked the oysters, roughly chop up eight of them and set the other four aside. Next, put the cooled, chopped oysters in a mixing bowl and mix with the blue cheese, parsley, breadcrumbs and butter. Place the mixture in clingfilm and roll into a thin sausage shape, then pop into the fridge to cool down. When the butter has set, cut into four equal pieces and then stuff each fillet pocket. Secure with a toothpick so it won't spill out when you braai it. Rub each fillet with salt, cracked black pepper and olive oil and set aside.

When your braai is ready (coals should be moderate to hot), braai the fillets for about 3 minutes a side. Remove from the grid and set aside for about 5 minutes, then slice diagonally in half and garnish with the extra oysters and a sprinkling of fresh parsley.

OSTRICH STEAK
with Béarnaise

FOR THE SAUCE:

½ red onion, finely chopped

4 tablespoons of white grape vinegar

4 tablespoons of water

1 bay leaf

2 teaspoons of dried tarragon

4 free-range egg yolks

¾ cup of melted butter

1 small handful of chopped chives

FOR THE STEAK:

200 g ostrich steak

cracked black pepper

coarse sea salt

olive oil

BY *Tippie & Santie*

This is a French classic with a Karoo twist. The secret is in the sauce and getting it juuust right.

First up, start with the sauce. Place a pot over moderate coals then add the red onion, vinegar, water, bay leaf and tarragon. Slowly bring to a simmer and then reduce the sauce by half. Remove from the heat and set aside to cool as much as possible, while you make a hollandaise. In a glass bowl, whisk together the egg yolks then slowly add the melted butter while still whisking. The butter must be cool enough to not cook the eggs. Once you've added and whisked in all the yolks, mix in a little bit of your cooled tarragon vinegar then add the sauce to a pan. Place over a very low heat and slowly stir in about three more tablespoons of tarragon vinegar, and stir until the sauce has thickened. Again – keep a close eye on the heat of the coals – if it's too hot the sauce will curdle, and then you'll have to start from scratch, again. Once thickened, remove the sauce from the heat, stir in the chives, have a taste and adjust the seasoning.

While you're busy in the last stages of the béarnaise sauce, get your friend to start on the steaks: Roll the meat in plenty of cracked black pepper, sprinkle salt to taste and then lightly drizzle olive oil over the steak. Heat a pan over moderate coals and then sear the steaks on all sides for about 1 minute on each side (you want the steak to be rare – if you prefer it cooked longer, then go for it). Remove from the pan and let it rest for about 5 minutes before plating up.

Serve the steak, drizzled with the béarnaise sauce and a fresh salad on the side. This dish is even better when you pair it with a glass (or three) of KWV Chardonnay. Lekker!

WELLINGTON

BY *Yusuf & Stephen*

For the crepes, YOU NEED:

1 cup of cake flour

½ teaspoon of baking powder

1 free-range egg

¾ cup of water

2 tablespoons of canola oil

For the pâté, YOU NEED:

a couple of knobs of butter

1 large onion, finely chopped

2 cloves garlic, crushed and chopped

a couple of sprigs of fresh thyme

200 g chicken livers

a splash of KWV Brandy

100 ml fresh cream

salt and pepper to taste

a small handful of fresh parsley, chopped

FOR THE REST:

1 roll of puff pastry

4 ostrich fillet steaks

1 free-range egg, beaten

A traditional Wellington. Done on a braai. Move over England, we've got this! We might not be great at football, but certain things – like rugby and how to actually cook meat – should be left to the ones who know how to do it.

Start off by making the crêpes. Mix together all the ingredients until you have a lump-free batter. Grease a fireproof pan, place over moderate to hot coals and, once hot, scoop a spoonful of batter inside. Thinly spread the mixture by swirling the pan. Once cooked on the one side (this shouldn't take more than a minute or two) flip the crêpe and cook the other side. Keep repeating until you've used up all the batter. There will probably be a couple of extra ones so, if you want to, sprinkle with cinnamon sugar and have a quick snack.

Once your crêpes are done, it's time to make the chicken liver pâté. Heat a fireproof pan over moderate to hot coals, add a knob of butter and sauté the onion until soft, then stir through the garlic and thyme. Next, add the chicken livers and, just before they're cooked through (about 10 minutes), pour in a shot of brandy and flambé. Once the flames have died down, pour in the cream, let it simmer for a couple more minutes or until the sauce has thickened slightly. Remove the livers from the heat and season to taste. While they're still hot, blitz them in a blender or if you don't have a blender, chop them very finely and stir through another knob of butter and chopped fresh parsley. If you want the pâté to be a little richer, add some cream cheese.

And now the rest. You're going to make four individual Wellingtons using the four steaks. Roll out the sheet of puff pastry – as thinly as you can and big enough to cover each steak –then lay a crêpe on top of each pastry. Generously spread pâté over the crêpes, then place an ostrich fillet steak on top of each crêpe. Roll the pastry over so that you cover the whole steak, then tuck in the edges and brush with egg wash to secure in place. Put the Wellies to the side to rest (if you don't, the puff pastry will shrink when you bake it).

After about 20 minutes, pop them into a kassie (see page 126) and bake over moderate coals until golden brown – but be careful you don't overdo it, you want the fillet to be medium (at most).

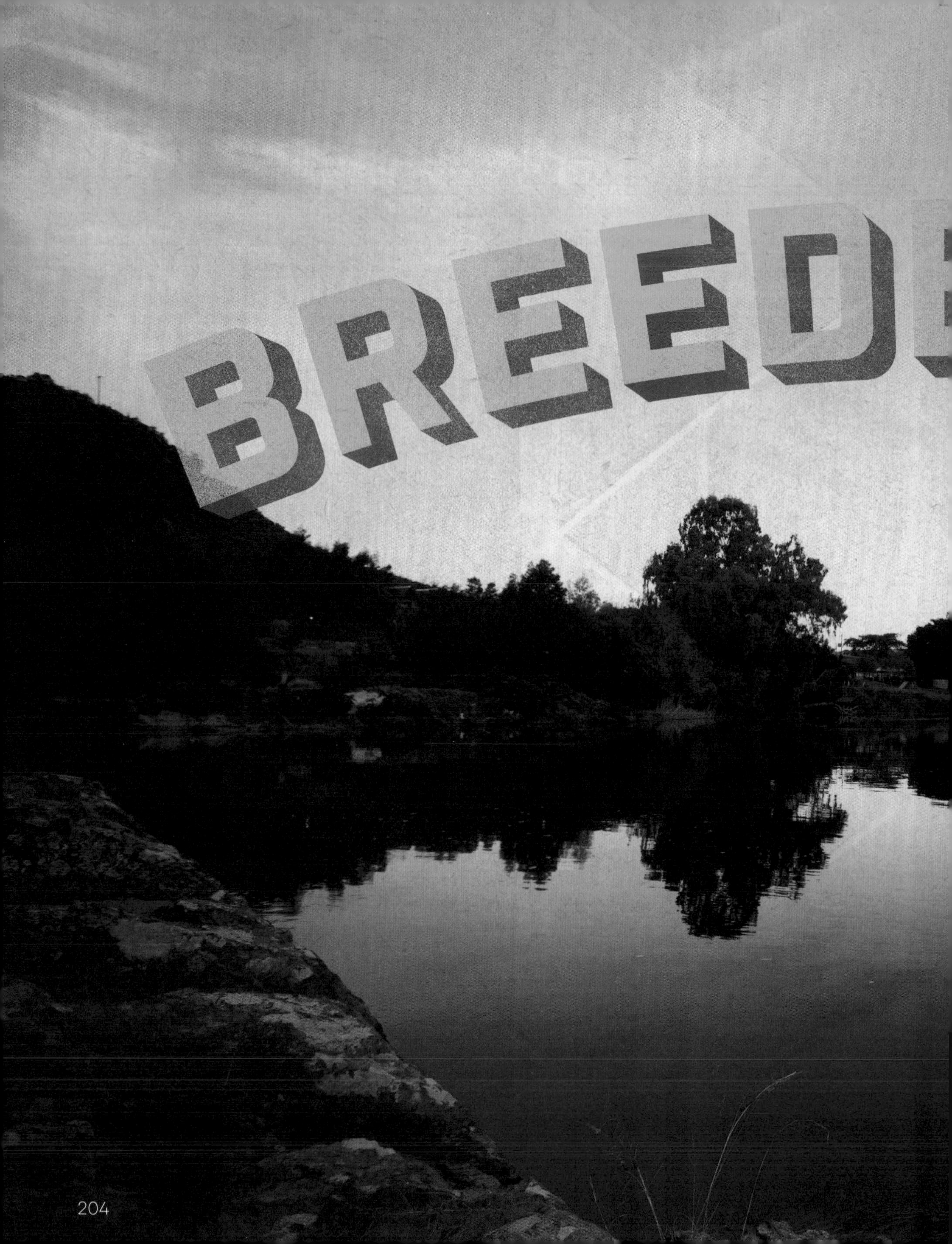
BREED

This was it. We had travelled 9 000 kilometres, spent 70-odd days together and in-between all the work that had to get done along the way, we ate like kings (mostly) and drank a whole load of brandy and cokes. This was our final destination of what had been one of the most incredible and memorable adventures. Our journey had started in the Cape of Storms and saw us travelling up the east coast and across to the rough seas of the west coast, then alongside southern Africa's biggest river, through the desolate moonscapes and painted landscapes of Namibia, its ancient deserts and the edge of Africa's biggest canyon, through the thirsty land of the Tankwa Karoo, over the most picturesque passes and now, finally here, a mere two hours from Cape Town.

Oddly enough, it felt like I had come full circle. You see, many moons ago, I came to the Felix Unite Round the Bend Camp while I was shooting the first episode of my very first show called *Cooked*. Back then I was younger (much), more raucous, still single and pretty much just behaving badly. Case in point? My favourite memory of this place was setting the bar on fire. Literally. It. Was. Great.

The lodge is situated on the banks of the Breede River and there's a saying that goes something like 'if you want to find your way home, follow the river' and this seemed apt for us. (Well at least for those of us who come from Cape Town.) First we had to get through three more days of filming, but we had a carrot dangling in front of us: the wrap party. This would be the last fire we would light on our trip and we were all excited to wrap things up and to finally go back home. But anyone in the film industry will know that at the end of any show or film, comes the wrap party. And because these types of parties tend to go on right through the night, I think it's only right that we end our journey with some party food.

PIZZA TIME

If you've followed our braai journey for the last two years, you'll know that making a pizza on the braai is one of our favourite things to do. I first did it years and years ago in my first TV series, *Cooked*. Then, many years later, Bertus did it on the braai, straight on the fire. This time around, we created a new toy, which we called a pizza box. And while I would love to wax lyrical about how genius this is, it's actually just some common sense. And when you get it right, braaied pizza is a great, sociable party food where everyone gets to make their own. Just be sure to make a few pizza box ovens and have a big braai area.

To make your pizza box, YOU NEED:

1 box (intact) – a medium-sized one

1 roll of tinfoil

1 unglazed terracotta tile

Place the unglazed terracotta tile on the grid over moderate to hot coals.

Line the inside and the edges of the box with foil – shiny side out. Once the tile is hot, sprinkle with flour, place your pizza on top and cover with the box. You've now created a little bush pizza oven. Simple!

PS: You can cook other things inside your little bush-oven too – think about trying a roast chicken this way. And please let me know how it turns out.

The GREEN Genie

BY *Justin Bonello*

This pizza is inspired by a salad that my wife makes, which I absolutely love. I made this the first time for a charity event for Col'Cacchio and it made it onto their menu – it's *that* good. Incidentally, this is also where I met Bertus for the first time and we became friends.

PIZZA DOUGH:

500 g wholewheat or white bread flour

a big pinch of salt

1 x 10 g sachet instant yeast

325 ml warm water

Combine the flour and salt in a large mixing bowl. Activate and dissolve the yeast by placing it in a bowl and adding the warm water. Give it a stir, and sprinkle a handful of flour over the mixture to prevent the yeast from forming a crust. Leave the yeast mixture in a warm spot for about 10 minutes or until it begins to froth. Gradually add it to the flour, mixing it well until it forms a dough. The only way to do this is with your hands. If the dough is too sticky, add a bit more flour; if it's too dry, add a splash more water, and so on. Knead for 10 minutes until the dough has a smooth, elastic consistency. Sprinkle some flour onto your work surface, place the dough on the flour and cover with a damp tea-towel. Leave the dough to rise for about 30 minutes or until it has doubled in size. In the meantime, light your braai fire and get started on making the pizza toppings and the tomato sauce for the base.

TOMATO SAUCE:

This is dead simple, and you don't need to precook it. All you do is take 1 x 410 g tin of whole peeled tomatoes, put them in a bowl and crush them with your hands, then add dried oregano, salt and pepper to taste.

• •

Drizzle the butternut cubes with olive oil, add the whole peeled garlic and wrap them in tinfoil, then roast them on moderate coals until the garlic is soft and the butternut starts caramelising on the edges. At the same time, on the same fire, put a pot of water on the boil and cook the beetroots for about 40 minutes. They should be cooked, but still crunchy. Cut off the tips, remove the skins and cut into small chunks. In a nonstick pan, dry-toast the pine nuts and all the seeds and then set aside.

• •

ASSEMBLE THE PIZZA:

Take a fistful of pizza dough and place it on a clean surface, sprinkled with flour. Roll it out (if you can get a round pizza base, well done. If not – it doesn't matter at all! Once the dough is rolled out (and keep in mind it has to fit onto the terracotta tile), sprinkle some flour over the tile surface and place the dough on top.

Now it's time to play with the toppings. First, spread some of the tomato sauce over the dough base – but not too much, otherwise your pizza will get soggy. Next, sprinkle over some mozzarella then add a couple of chunks of butternut and beetroot. Cut up some of that soft garlic and sprinkle over the veggies, along with all the toasted seeds. Top this with some Danish feta and you're done. Do a couple more – there's enough dough for this to make about six small pizzas.

Place the terracotta tile onto a braai grid over moderate coals and pop the box over the top. When the tile is hot, sprinkle some flour over the surface and put the pizza on top, covering with the pizza box again. The idea is that the heat will reflect against the foil on the inside and cook the pizza from the top and the coals underneath takes care of the pizza's bottom. Depending on the size of your braai and the box, you should be able to braai two pizzas at a time. When the cheese has melted and the crust is crispy and golden take the pizzas off the heat.

Garnish with fresh rocket and watercress and a drizzle of balsamic glaze.

TOPPINGS:

1 medium-sized butternut, peeled and cut into 1 cm cubes

a drizzle of olive oil

5–6 cloves garlic, peeled

4 or 5 medium-sized beetroots

a palmful of pine nuts

a small palmful of sesame seeds

a small palmful of pumpkin seeds

a handful of grated mozzarella

a handful of smooth Danish feta, cut into smallish chunks

a double handful of watercress

a double handful of rocket

a drizzle of balsamic glaze

211

Crew Pizzas

And then this happened. And it was cheesy and delicious and the perfect in-between-shooting-a-show-snack. Make up your own, or try one of these combinations some of my crew conjured up.

. . . .

NICKI

Anyone who knows this girl, will know two things about her as fact. One, when she's having a really good *kuier*, her alter ego likes to come out to play, and his name is Rick. Two, she has a soft spot for the smelliest cheese of them all: blue cheese. In fact, she'll eat the entire thing by herself... and never gain any weight. That's probably her superhero power. *That...* and tackling people into shrubs.

Combo: *crumbled blue cheese, crispy bacon, fig preserve*

. . . .

MISHAL

He's the soft-spoken, shy, gentlemanly type. His taste in pizza topping absolutely does not reflect this though. This one is full of different flavours that will wake up your taste buds in a big way.

Combo: *avocado, blue cheese, piquant peppers, garlic, chilli, mozzarella*

ALICE

She's all classy and beautiful. And a little strange. So is her pizza.

Combo: *anchovies, black olives, mozzarella, fresh rosemary, fresh oregano*

. . . .

MEGAN T

She's one of the hardest workers on the crew. Really likes chilli. And lots of it! Probably keeps her awake.

Combo: *loads of chilli (sliced and seeds removed), a couple of cloves garlic (crushed), cherry tomatoes (halved), anchovies (kept whole), fresh rocket to garnish*

. . . .

DANIELA

Brilliant photographer and lover of good food, so it makes sense that her pizza topping is a little more complicated.

Combo: *chilli and garlic tomato base (just add chilli and garlic to the tomato base on page 211), anchovies (kept whole), chorizo (sliced), mozzarella*

Zanzibar Street Pizza

For the dough, YOU NEED:

300 g cake flour

250 ml water

2 tablespoons of sunflower oil, plus extra for frying

a pinch of salt

For the filling, YOU NEED:

100 g sliced mushrooms

1 onion, chopped

1 tomato, diced

2 carrots, julienned

2 tablespoons of chopped fresh parsley

1 bunch of asparagus, chopped

100 g grated Cheddar or mozzarella cheese

80 g cream cheese

2 free-range eggs, whisked

salt and black pepper

Bertus discovered these while on his honeymoon and made them his own back on South African soil. The taste? Well, imagine a quiche combined with a pizza. Exactly. It's a little bit of heaven. This is a killer pre-braai snack or light lunch.

Combine all the ingredients, mix well and then knead the dough until soft and elastic. Divide the dough into eight equal portions, roll into balls and allow to rest while you make the filling.

Mix together all the ingredients and season to taste. Take each ball of dough, and then roll it out as thin as you can. Place the filling in the centre and make little dough pouches.

Place a flat-bottom potjie over moderate coals and add a generous glug of cooking oil. Fry the parcels in batches, on both sides, until crisp and golden. Drain on kitchen paper.

BY *Bertus Basson*

Smoked Mackerel & Yellowtail SAMOOSAS

For the filling, YOU NEED:

smoked mackerel

leftover yellowtail

lemon zest

50 g chopped piquant peppers

40 g fresh coriander

40 g fresh chives

1 small red onion, finely chopped

20 g paprika

salt and pepper to taste

1 roll of phyllo pastry

TO FINISH:

1 cup of flour

4 tablespoons of water

oil for frying

Fishy samoosas are the perfect solution to leftover braaied fish.

Flake the fish and remove all the bones. In a large mixing bowl, add all the rest of the ingredients and mix well. Have a taste and season as needed.

Cut the phyllo into long strips of about 5 cm wide, then place them on a flat surface. Mix together 1 cup of flour and 4 tablespoons of water for the paste that you're going to use to stick the pastry together. Take roughly 1 teaspoon of the fishy filling and scoop it on the bottom left corner of the pastry. Lengthways, fold the phyllo pastry in the opposite direction to form a triangle shape – do this with every fold and before completing the last fold run some of the flour paste onto the inside of the pastry and secure. You should now have a perfectly shaped samoosa!

Heat some oil in a large pot over moderate to hot coals – but be careful not to burn the oil! Once the oil is piping hot, carefully place a couple of samoosas inside. Deep-fry them in batches until golden and crispy, then remove with a slotted spoon and drain on kitchen paper to get rid of the excess oil. Serve hot or cold.

BY *Yusuf & Stephen*

BY *Petrus Madutlela*

MOJITO

WHAT YOU NEED:

6 tablespoons of brown sugar

1 litre sparkling water

4 limes, cut into wedges

7 shots of white rum

1 bunch fresh mint

½ cup of ice

This was Petrus's solution to the morning-after-the-party drink. It's like his Bloody Mary. The hair of the dog. That fragile, desperate attempt to feel just a little bit better because, let's face it, you should have known better! You know what I'm talking about. We've all done it over a raucous weekend. Sometimes on a week night! HORROR! When you're in a city, finding a solution to your sore head is easy. But when you're in the middle of nowhere with no pain pills or hairy dogs in sight, and you've got nothing but a long day of relaxation ahead of you, mojitos are a refreshing pick-me-up for when you're feeling so dreadful you have no choice but to have a drink with your lunch. Or simply have it as cocktails on a hot summer night.

Stir together the brown sugar and sparkling water until the sugar dissolves. Add the lime wedges and the rum. Bruise the mint leaves too so that they release their flavour and add to the cocktail. Add the ice and pour into glasses and give to the worst, most thirsty looking friends around. Then send them back to bed. Or give them leftover *braaivleis*. If it's you, then go have a nap (after the mojito and leftovers, of course).

one BLOODY MARY.
just one....

YOU NEED:

about 5 tomatoes, chopped

½ onion, very finely chopped

salt and pepper to taste

1 shot of vodka

BY *Justin Bonello*

I discovered this by accident after returning to Cape Town. And it's so great and fresh. See it as a bonus recipe (like those hidden tracks on CDs – remember those?!).

Place the chopped tomatoes in a bowl. Add the chopped onion and season with salt and pepper. Leave it. What's happening is that the salt is drawing the moisture out of the tomatoes and creating the sweetest juice you will ever taste. This should be left to stand for about 1 hour. Pour the tomato salad into a colander and let the excess drip through into a bowl – give it some help by squashing the tomatoes with a spoon (or your hands if you really want to). Pour the tomato juice into a glass, add vodka and ice (both optional) and drink.

Oh, and use the tomato and onion to make a relish so it doesn't go to waste!

Lekker!

Thank You!

Of all the pages written in this book, this is probably the one I dread the most. Not because I'm unthankful, but because when you go on a journey for the extent of time that we do, the list of people to remember to thank becomes longer and longer with every kilometre we travel. So if I leave anyone out, please know that it's not because I'm an ungracious, unthankful SOB, but just because I'm human... and my mind's already on the next journey.

So, in no particular order of importance, here goes nothing!

As always, to my long suffering wife Eugenie, my three children, Dan, Sam and Gabriella – for keeping me going when the tunnel was dark and when it appeared like there was no light. To Mom - Bean there is no 'my story' without you - enough said. To my old man Charly – for introducing me to the road and wide-open spaces. My sister Tanya and her family, Dimitri, and little IceCake... for keeping me grounded.

Then there are the actual rock stars of my journeys. To my business partner, Peter Gird

and The Ultimate Braai Master Crew – all 70 of you! You're the guys and girls who just get it, who work tirelessly to make the crazy ideas I have an actuality that we get to share with the world. To all of you my deepest most heartfelt thanks. I know I fight, that sometimes I'm probably not the easiest cat in the world – but you're all always welcome around my fire... please say I'm welcome around yours...

PS: See if you can spot yourselves in this picture of that night we'll always remember as our little AfricaBurn.

To the team at Penguin Random House. In the beginning it felt like the year was full of turmoil... then Steve and Linda – you stepped in, a breath of fresh air, took control, made me feel like I was at home with a family. Thank you for the trust and faith – it's now seven books and counting. And then there's Jean Fryer – full of go and zest – to all of you - thank you for making a life dream of mine come true. Special thanks to Joy Clack, Beverley Dodd and Samantha Fick for your immaculate eye for detail.

To Caro Gardner – I have in my mind, pictures of you always going the extra mile – and somehow, making potjie pots sexy. You are the bestest.

Then to Louis Hiemstra, Daniela Zondagh and Sunel Haasbroek. Three talented photographers, all with an eye for art and the journey. My memories of all these trips and the trips to come would not be complete without your view of my world.

Oh, and that girl, I forget her name, that writes like a man but is a girl. Who never misses a deadline, who is conscientious, humble and beautiful – I'm so glad that years ago you gave up writing trade mags and took a leap of faith with me – Helena Lombard, writer extraordinaire – it takes a bunch of us to do these journeys – but only you have the skill to make my mayhem real and written on these pages.

Bertus Basson and Petrus Madutlela. Lads – friendships that form for life from such humble beginnings. I look forward to our early morning clear-our-head walks and that magic that happens with food when you chuck us into a big potjie pot and stir.

Quint and Toby of Twoshoes. Toby– I got to break your virginity with this one bud and I must say to the two of you – you've been on this journey with me from day one – and you still make it amazing... every single time.

Thanks to our gracious hosts we met along our journey for putting up with this crazy circus: Monkey Valley Resort, Breede River Resort and Fishing Lodge, Rondeberg Resort, Bulshoek Dam Resort, Noup Diamond Cottages, Die Houthoop, Felix Unite Provenance Camp, Taleni Group Properties (Sossusvlei Lodge and Desert Camp), Khamkirri Private Game Reserve, Tankwa Tented Camp, Buffelsdrift Game Lodge and Felix Unite Round the Bend. Oh and thanks to Colemans for keeping our beers nice and cold along the way!

To all the teams who travelled with us for two months and who shared your recipes, thank you! I hope that in some small way you've become travel addicts like the rest of us!

And last but very definitely not least, there's you. That person who picks up my books and thumbs through them... feels that there's something written in these pages that resonates. Thank you for taking this journey with me and my crazy crew – truth is, without you – there is no me.

Justin Bonello

221

Recipe Index

MMA 2018

Written by Paul D. Gibson
Designed by Lucy Boyd

PBR

A Pillar Box Red Publication

© 2017. Published by Pillar Box Red Publishing Limited, in association with The Daily Mirror. Printed in the EU.

ISBN 978-1-9997489-0-6

Images © PA Images, Getty Images and Shutterstock.

CONTENTS

INTRODUCTION

Welcome to Mirror Sport MMA 2018. This book takes a closer look at Mixed Martial Arts, the fastest growing and most exciting sport in the world.

It will take you back to Ancient Greece to trace the evolution of MMA from Pankration to today's UFC superstars via everything from Wrestling, Judo and Bruce Lee in-between. Then learn about the first ever Ultimate Fighting Championship which took place twenty-five years ago in Colorado.

For the uninitiated, there is a breakdown of the different martial arts skills needed to survive in the Octagon, as well as a rundown of the key techniques and moves that today's champions employ.

Speaking of champions, profiles of all eleven can be found within, alongside in-depth looks at legends of the sport such as Anderson Silva, Chuck Liddell, Jon Jones and Ronda Rousey. Some of those stars feature in the Classic Fights section, a walk down memory lane to revisit a selection of the most epic battles ever seen in an MMA arena.

2017 will be remembered for Floyd Mayweather versus Conor McGregor, the biggest event in combat sports history. This book analyses the differences between MMA and boxing and then reviews the fight, hype and crazy behind-the-scenes build-up which led to the two men squaring off in the ring.

There are also quizzes and puzzles to test your MMA knowledge and the entire publication is filled with great pictures of all your favourite fighters.

What more could you want as an MMA fan!

CONOR MCGREGOR

McGregor grew up in the south Dublin suburb of Crumlin where he played football for a local team. At the age of twelve he started boxing at former Irish Olympian Phil Sutcliffe's gym, and his love for fighting flourished. He was an accomplished amateur boxer, but by his mid-teens he was already being drawn to the world of mixed martial arts.

When he left school he began an apprenticeship to become a plumber, but it killed him that every minute he spent fixing pipes was a minute away from the MMA gym. A chat with Ireland's first UFC fighter Tom Egan convinced him to dedicate his life to fighting, so in 2007 he fought one amateur bout and then turned pro.

In 2008, McGregor linked up with John Kavanagh, the head coach of Straight Blast Gym in Dublin, and began refining the skills which would eventually take him to the very top of the MMA ladder. Boxing had taught him how to throw a punch and judge range and distance, so the pair focused on Jiu-Jitsu in order to give Conor a grappling game when needed.

McGregor made his pro debut in March of 2008 and as he learnt his trade he actually lost two of his first six fights, both to submissions. But the God-given power in his left hand helped him win the other four by knockout and then embark on a five-year, fifteen-fight unbeaten run. Along the way he became the first man in Cage Warrior's history to hold two belts simultaneously when he claimed the featherweight and lightweight straps in 2012.

In early 2013, UFC President Dana White was in Ireland and reported being inundated with requests to offer McGregor a contract with the organisation. White didn't need much convincing and in April of that year Conor stepped into the Octagon for the first time to stop Marcus Brimmage with a barrage of punches barely a minute into the opening round.

Notorious was up and running and he refused to look back. He clearly beat current UFC featherweight kingpin Max Holloway in a unanimous decision before battering the Brazilian Diego Brandao in front of a raucous home crowd in Dublin. Dustin Poirier was next, but the top-ten ranked featherweight lasted less than two minutes. McGregor by now already had his sights firmly set on the champion Jose Aldo and when he easily defeated Dennis Siver at UFC Fight Night 59, he was granted his shot.

An Aldo injury postponed that bout, and afforded McGregor time to stop Chad Mendes in the second round at UFC 189, but the inevitable occurred at UFC 194 when Conor knocked Aldo out in just thirteen seconds to fulfil his destiny. He had one gold

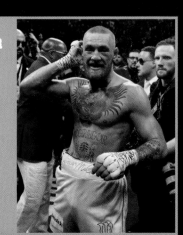

NAME: CONOR "NOTORIOUS" MCGREGOR

FROM: DUBLIN, IRELAND

HEIGHT: 5' 9"

MMA RECORD: 21-3

DIVISION: 155LB LIGHTWEIGHT CHAMPION

BACKGROUND: BOXING AND JIU-JITSU

UFC belt around his waist, but he immediately wanted another. The lightweight champion Rafael dos Anjos was the target, but once again a Brazilian champ withdrew a few weeks out from a fight against Notorious.

Nate Diaz emerged as an opponent to allow Conor to headline UFC 196 as planned, but now it was a non-title bout at 170lbs rather than a 155lb fight for a title. Diaz's extra weight proved decisive as he weathered McGregor's early storm before submitting the Irishman towards the end of the second. It was a first defeat since November 2010, but little time was wasted in seeking revenge as Conor beat Nate over five epic rounds just five months later.

There was still time in 2016 for McGregor to squeeze in one more fight, and this time the lightweight crown was up for grabs. Conor made no mistake, outclassing new champion Eddie Alvarez with a dazzling array of accurate striking to stop the brave American mid-way through the second round and become the first fighter in UFC history to hold two titles simultaneously.

As famous for his quick wit and brash personality as for his unique ability at fighting, McGregor was now the biggest superstar in combat sports. He used his gifts to transcend MMA and enter the world of mainstream celebrity like no male fighter ever had before.

Conor took some time off in early 2017 for the arrival of his first child, but it wasn't long before he was back, this time in a boxing ring rather than an Octagon for the fight of the century against Floyd Mayweather. In his professional boxing debut, McGregor managed to take an all-time great into the tenth round before the referee stopped the fight. It was yet another remarkable performance from a man that continues making the impossible achievable and we all hold our breath awaiting his next career move.

A brief history of MMA

Although the term Mixed Martial Arts did not appear in print until a review of the inaugural Ultimate Fighting Championship at the end of 1993, the sport, in one form or another, has been in existence for over 2,500 years.

The Ancient Greek discipline of Pankration is regarded as the earliest modern-day MMA precursor. As far back as the year 600 BC, Greek men were stripping naked, covering themselves in sand to increase grip, and using a combination of wrestling and striking in fights that frequently ended in death.

Fast forward a thousand years and you'll find medieval Japanese Samurais developing the martial art of Jujutsu as a means to grapple and overpower an enemy wearing armour against whom kicks and punches were totally ineffective.

By the late 1800s, Jujutsu was streamlined into Judo before that discipline combined with European Catch Wrestling to provide the inspiration for the Brazilian art of Jiu-Jitsu, a gi-based grappling style. The renowned Gracie family were the forerunners of this new form of fighting and they used it to dominate the no-holds-barred contests known as Vale Tudo (anything goes) that grew in popularity throughout the twentieth century.

Meanwhile, a young Bruce Lee was leaving his own indelible mark on the evolution of martial arts in California. Initially trained in Wing Chun,

Lee soon saw the disadvantages of being restricted to one particular discipline in an open fight. He therefore bypassed labelling different styles and instead created his own philosophy called Jeet Kune Do, or Way of the Intercepting Fist. His belief was that each person should develop their own individual means to win a fight, an idea which can be seen as the cornerstone of modern MMA.

Rorion Gracie then introduced Jiu-Jitsu to the US in the early 1980s when he issued his Gracie Challenge to take on any other fighting discipline and win using his family's martial art. At the same time in Japan, their version of professional wrestling had developed into a genuine fighting sport and was soon joined by a wrestling hybrid called Shoot Fighting and an aggressive form of Karate known in English as Combat Karate.

All of the above, plus practitioners of traditional Boxing, Kickboxing, Sumo Wrestling, Taekwondo, and Savate then met in Colorado in November of 1993 at the first Ultimate Fighting Championship. Royce Gracie took little time submitting every foe he faced to claim the title and prove Jiu-Jitsu to be the dominant force in mixed martial arts.

But MMA is an ever evolving multi-disciplined pursuit and it wasn't long before fighters

" TODAY MMA IS IN AN ERA IN WHICH THE MOST EFFECTIVE AND DEVASTATING STRIKERS ARE ENJOYING A LOT OF SUCCESS "

developed ways to defend, counter and defeat the best pure Jiu-Jitsu players. Wrestlers came to the fore with their ground and pound game, before they in turn were bested by the sprawl and brawlers who learnt to resist takedowns and keep the action on feet. Today MMA is in an era in which the most effective and devastating strikers are enjoying a lot of success, but who knows what style is currently being perfected in a gym to move the sport forward once more.

FAMOUS FANS

Answers on page 60-61

Can you name these famous fans?

1.......................

2.......................

3.......................

4.......................

5.......................

6.......................

7.............................

8.............................

9.............................

10.............................

11.............................

12.............................

13.............................

14.............................

15.............................

16.............................

17.............................

18.............................

WORDSEARCH

Find the words in the grid. Words can go horizontally, vertically and diagonally in all eight directions.

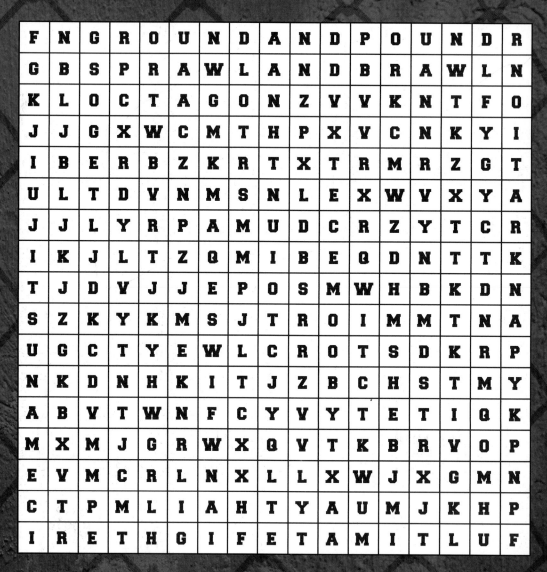

F	N	G	R	O	U	N	D	A	N	D	P	O	U	N	D	R
G	B	S	P	R	A	W	L	A	N	D	B	R	A	W	L	N
K	L	O	C	T	A	G	O	N	Z	V	V	K	N	T	F	O
J	J	G	X	W	C	M	T	H	P	X	V	C	N	K	Y	I
I	B	E	R	B	Z	K	R	T	X	T	R	M	R	Z	G	T
U	L	T	D	V	N	M	S	N	L	E	X	W	V	X	Y	A
J	J	L	Y	R	P	A	M	U	D	C	R	Z	Y	T	C	R
I	K	J	L	T	Z	Q	M	I	B	E	Q	D	N	T	T	K
T	J	D	V	J	J	E	P	O	S	M	W	H	B	K	D	N
S	Z	K	Y	K	M	S	J	T	R	O	I	M	M	T	N	A
U	G	C	T	Y	E	W	L	C	R	O	T	S	D	K	R	P
N	K	D	N	H	K	I	T	J	Z	B	C	H	S	T	M	Y
A	B	V	T	W	N	F	C	Y	V	Y	T	E	T	I	Q	K
M	X	M	J	G	R	W	X	Q	V	T	K	B	R	V	O	P
E	V	M	C	R	L	N	X	L	L	X	W	J	X	G	M	N
C	T	P	M	L	I	A	H	T	Y	A	U	M	J	K	H	P
I	R	E	T	H	G	I	F	E	T	A	M	I	T	L	U	F

Greco Roman

Ground and Pound

Iceman

Jedrzejczyk

Jiu Jitsu

Muay Thai

Octagon

Pankration

Rowdy

Sprawl and Brawl

Submission

The Spider

Ultimate Fighter

Wrestling

Answers on page 60-61

STIPE MIOCIC

Miocic was born and raised in the US but both of his parents are from Croatia. He has always been a gifted athlete and played baseball, American football and wrestled in high school. He continued playing baseball in college and several MLB franchises were interested in offering him a contract. But Miocic was drawn to combat sports and decided to concentrate on wrestling, eventually reaching NCAA division one.

Towards the end of college, Miocic began boxing and would go on to become the Cleveland Golden Gloves champion. The Croatian legend Mirko Cro Cop was at this time one of the biggest names in the UFC and that inspired Miocic to try MMA.

With six straight victories, five by KO, Miocic won the North American Allied Fight Series heavyweight champion and earned a spot in the UFC. When he won his first fight in the Octagon he was still working as a firefighter and paramedic in Ohio, but he soon decided to focus all of his time and energy on MMA.

The decision was a wise one and Miocic was soon racking up performance of the night, knockout of the night, and fight of the night bonuses. In May 2015 he defeated Mark Hunt and embarked on a run that has seen him stop some stellar names. Amongst them, Fabricio Werdum, when Miocic took the Brazilian's heavyweight title in front of his own fans. Alistair Overeem and Junior Dos Santos have since tried and failed to take the prized belt from Stipe.

NAME:
STIPE MIOCIC

FROM:
OHIO, USA

HEIGHT:
6' 4"

MMA RECORD:
17-2

DIVISION:
HEAVYWEIGHT CHAMPION

BACKGROUND:
WRESTLING AND BOXING

DAN HENDERSON V
MAURICIO RUA UFC 139

Dan "Hendo" Henderson is one of the greatest mixed martial artists the world has ever seen. An Olympic wrestler, he added Boxing and Muay Thai to his arsenal before embarking on a twenty-year career in which he beat a total of seventeen MMA world champions and was himself a multiple world title holder.

Mauricio "Shogun" Rua hails from Curitiba in Brazil where he grew up training in Jiu-Jitsu and Muay Thai. He began his fighting career in the no-holds-barred Vale Tudo contests of his home country before rising to become Pride middleweight champion in Japan and the UFC's light heavyweight king.

The two men were legendary figures in Pride and when the Japanese promotion merged with the UFC in 2007, both were welcomed into the Octagon with open arms. They operated in different weight classes for most of their careers, but when Hendo grew into a light heavyweight the UFC couldn't wait to match them together. The bout headlined UFC 139 in California and was even better than everyone believed it would be.

ROUND ONE

The action was incredible from the off. After exchanging blows, Rua was caught in a guillotine that Henderson held then released with a knee to the face. Rua was bloodied after only a minute and soon he was dropped by a big right hand. Hendo then threw his opponent onto the canvas with disdain and although he was briefly down himself, it was clearly the American's round.

ROUND TWO

The second was a more even affair as both recovered from the frenetic pace of the opener. It was most notable for the moments when both stood their ground, planted their feet and swung from the hips. They each landed, but neither clean enough to force a knockdown or knockout.

ROUND THREE

Hendo landed a vicious inside leg kick early in the third and followed up with a booming right hand which dropped Shogun. Henderson then detonated a series of bombs on his downed opponent as the referee hovered, close to stepping in. Somehow Rua survived, but both men were exhausted from their efforts.

ROUND FOUR

The biggest punch of the fourth was a monster uppercut from Rua which seemed to have Henderson out on his feet. It led to a successful takedown for the Brazilian, but as he tried to batter Hendo from a full mount position and then secure a rear-naked choke, the American incredibly rolled out and reversed it to stay alive.

ROUND FIVE

Henderson's 41 years were now catching up with him as he gasped for oxygen throughout the final five minutes while Rua, more than ten years younger than his rival, pushed hard for the finish he knew he needed. Hendo took plenty of punishment when Shogun mounted him, but managed to hold on for a unanimous 48-47 victory. Dana White described it as one of the top three greatest fights in UFC history.

The First
ULTIMATE FIGHTING CHAMPIONSHIP

The Gracie family dreamt up the inaugural Ultimate Fighting Championship as a way to prove that Brazilian Jiu-Jitsu was the most effective fighting style. Royce was to represent the Gracies while seven other competitors were invited to the knockout tournament in Colorado to compete for the $50,000 first prize on live PPV television. Sumo, Savate, Kickboxing, Boxing, Karate, Shootfighting and Taekwondo were all represented.

Described as a no-holds-barred contest, the tournament posters claimed that there were no rules to each fight. In fact, three moves were forbidden: biting, eye gouging and deliberate attacks to the groin. But other than that, the competitors were free to do whatever they wanted to knockout, submit or cause the opposition corner to throw in a white towel in defeat. There were also no judges, no time limits, no weight classes and the referee was not permitted to stop the fight. All the action took place in a specially-designed Octagon cage, exactly like the UFC fights of today.

UFC 1 got off to a brutal and bloody start when a 400lb pound sumo wrestler named Teila Tuli charged a Dutch kickboxer and savate expert called Gerard Gordeau. Gordeau landed an uppercut on the onrushing Tuli and then kicked the big man in the face as he floundered on his hands and knees. One of Tuli's teeth flew into the crowd and another embedded in Gordeau's foot.

The second bout was a stand-up war as kickboxing champion Kevin Rosier and Karate specialist Zane Frazier went toe-to-toe. Frazier's corner stopped the contest when their man fell to the canvas and Rosier began stomping on his head.

Next up was Royce against a nervous-looking light heavyweight boxer by the name of Art Jimmerson. Jimmerson, who had no idea what he had signed up for, appeared wearing one boxing glove and froze in front of Royce who easily took him down and submitted him. The formidable looking shootfighter Ken Shamrock then took on the equally imposing Taekwondo player Patrick Smith. Shamrock wasted little time in taking Smith down and submitting him with a heel lock.

In the semi-finals, Gordeau overwhelmed Rosier with leg kicks and elbows to claim victory inside a minute before the much anticipated match-up between Royce and Shamrock. Jiu-Jitsu and shootfighting were then regarded as the two most effective styles in MMA and finally the world would see two of their best practitioners battle it out. The fight was all over in 58 seconds, however, as Shamrock missed an attempted foot lock and Royce punished him with a gi choke that drew the submission.

The final was just as straight forward for the Jiu-Jitsu specialist as a battered and bruised Gordeau quickly found himself losing consciousness from a rear-naked choke. The Dutchman tapped frantically to indicate his submission, but Royce held on an extra few seconds to prolong the pain. It later transpired that the Brazilian was punishing his foe for an earlier illegal ear bite.

UFC 1 was a success for Jiu-Jitsu, but work was needed if MMA was to become a mainstream sport. This was achieved by Dana White and Lorenzo and Frank Fertitta when they bought the UFC and set about polishing and modernising the sport. The establishment of the Unified Rules of Mixed Martial Arts and the securing of sanctioning for MMA fights from the Nevada State Athletic Commission are two of the advancements which have gone a long way towards MMA becoming accepted as a legitimate sport.

MMA V BOXING: THE KEY DIFFERENCES

MMA	BOXING
Fights take place in an Octagon enclosed by a cage	Fights take place in a square boxing ring enclosed by ropes
Fighters wear 4 oz gloves	Fighters wear 8 or 10 oz gloves
Championship fights last for five x five minute rounds	Championship fights last for twelve x three minute rounds
A fighter may use every part of their body other than their head to attack an opponent	A fighter may only use his fists to attack an opponent
MMA is multi-disciplined sport incorporating elements of wrestling, boxing, kickboxing and all of the martial arts	Boxing is a single-disciplined sport
The fight continues on the ground	The fight stops when one of the boxers is knocked to the ground
Victory is awarded via decision, submission or knockout	Victory is awarded via decision or knockout

ANDERSON SILVA

Known as The Spider, Anderson Silva is widely regarded as the most complete mixed martial artist of all time. In fact, before MMA was even a recognised term, Silva was busy collecting all the diverse skills required to master the new form of fighting.

Born into poverty in the Brazilian city of Curitiba, Silva's parents initially couldn't afford to pay for Jiu-Jitsu lessons and so their son began learning by simply observing other neighbourhood kids practising. It wasn't until his teens that he was able to train properly and he then immediately set about mastering every discipline he came across.

By the time he was finished accumulating ranks, Silva was a black prajied in Muay Thai, a 3rd degree black belt in Jiu-Jitsu, a black belt in Judo, a 5th dan black belt in Taekwondo, a yellow rope in Capoeira and an accomplished professional boxer. He was also ready to dominate the world of MMA for more than a decade.

Before he entered the UFC, Silva wisely spent almost nine years refining his aggressive, multi-faceted counter-attacking style in a range of promotions from Brazil to the UK via Japan. Along the way he compiled a 17-4 record and claimed the Shooto middleweight championship in Osaka and the Cage Rage middleweight crown in London. The Spider then decided it was time to bring his talent to the Octagon.

His debut was an eliminator for the middleweight title against Chris Leben, then on a five-fight winning streak in the UFC. Silva peppered Leben with punches from the outset before knocking him out with a knee in under a minute. Rick Franklin was the champion and had only lost once in twenty-four contests, but The Spider needed less than three minutes to stop him and claim his crown.

So began Silva's incredible six year, sixteen-fight unbeaten run in which he defended his title a record ten times. But beyond the bare statistics, it was the moments of awe-inspiring fighting genius that cemented the Brazilian's place at the top of everyone's pound-for-pound list.

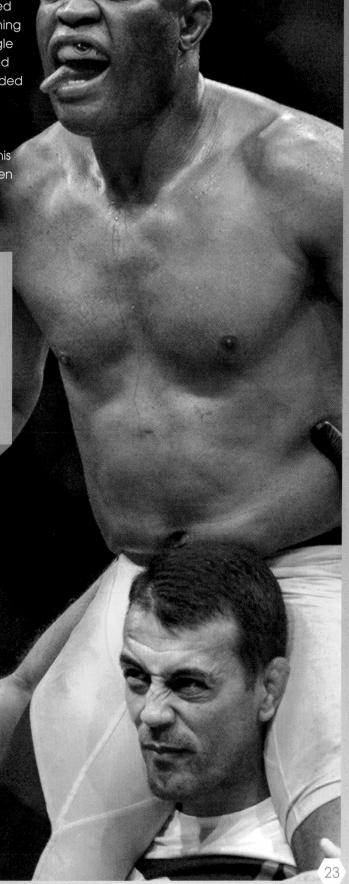

The innocuous-looking jab to an onrushing Forrest Griffin's chin that knocked the light-heavyweight champ out cold. Catching James Irwin's leg kick and knocking him out with a straight right hand all-in-one fluid motion. The front kick out of nowhere to the face of Vitor Belfort that ended that much anticipated match-up in the opening round. Submitting Chael Sonnen with a triangle armbar in the closing minutes of the fifth round when it looked like The Spider was finally headed for a loss in the Octagon. They are all iconic moments in UFC history.

Time finally caught up with Silva when he lost his title to Chris Weidman at the age of 38 and then suffered a horrific leg break in the rematch. A natural-born fighter, he is still competing in the UFC, two decades after his MMA debut.

NAME: ANDERSON "THE SPIDER" SILVA

FROM: CURITIBA, BRAZIL

HEIGHT: 6' 2"

MMA RECORD: 34-8, 1 NC

DIVISION: 185LB

BACKGROUND: MUAY THAI, JIU-JITSU, BOXING, JUDO, TAEKWONDO AND CAPOEIRA

CROSSWORD

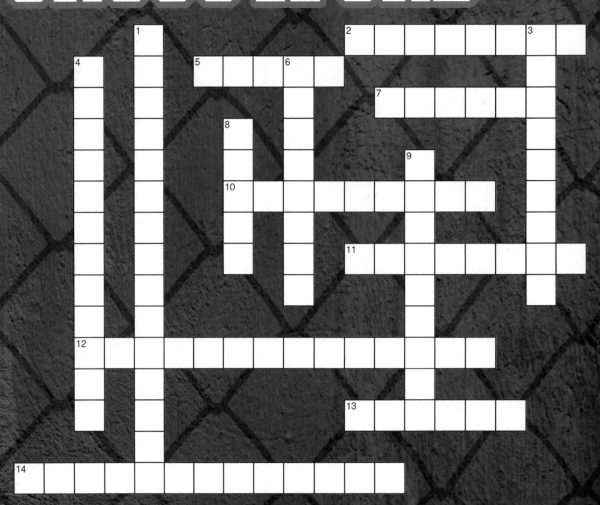

ACROSS

2   Surname of the brothers who bought the UFC in 2001

5   Surname of the UFC President

7   Brazilian Jiu-Jitsu family dynasty

10 Conor McGregor's nickname

11 City where UFC 1 took place

12 Move Nate Diaz used to submit Conor McGregor

13 Ronda Rousey's favourite submission

14 Brazilian MMA legend

DOWN

1   Boxer McGregor fought in the fight of the century

3   Korean martial art

4   Original champion of women's strawweight division

6   Number of seconds McGregor need to knockout Jose Aldo

8   Jon Jones' nickname

9   Fighter who inflicted first UFC loss on Ronda Rousey

Answers on page 60-61

Conor
McGregor

MMA TRAINING AND TECHNIQUES

Today's UFC stars are all professional athletes who dedicate themselves to the sport full-time. In the past, fighters would have travelled to different gyms and different coaches in order to train in various disciplines of combat. But there is now a movement towards the MMA factory model whereby fighters can train in every style they wish under one roof. In these specialist mixed martial arts gyms, UFC fighters are able to practise and perfect their skills in a wide range of fighting styles. Below is a selection of the most important styles to master if you are to be successful inside the Octagon.

BRAZILIAN JIU-JITSU

The Gracie family's contribution the world of MMA is a system of fighting that emphasises grappling and ground fighting. Jiu-Jitsu focuses on technique and utilising leverage in order to apply joint-locks and choke-holds to submit an opponent.

WRESTLING

Wrestling is an umbrella term to cover a variety of sports with Greco-Roman and Freestyle being perhaps the most relevant to MMA. Greco-Roman is what you see in the Olympics and forbids attacking below the waist, instead utilising throwing and slamming techniques. Freestyle on the other hand is all about shooting for the legs to take down an opponent. Both versions help MMA fighters in clinches.

JUDO

While the hip toss and other throws we see in the Octagon are clearly a result of Judo training, this martial art also brings a series of locks, chokes and strikes to the table.

BOXING

Boxing is all about perfecting the art of effective striking with the fist. All of the jabs, uppercuts, crosses and hooks you see in the Octagon originate in the boxing ring.

MUAY THAI

Referred to as the Art of Eight Limbs, Muay Thai training is why MMA fighters are adept at using their knees, elbow and shins as well as fists when they attack an opponent. It also introduces its own clinches to an MMA fighter's repertoire.

KEY MOVES AND TECHNIQUES

GROUND AND POUND

The process of taking an opponent down, securing a dominant top position, and then unleashing a barrage of punches and elbows. Mark Coleman is often credited with bringing this style to the UFC.

GUARD

When a fighter is on his back but is able to control his opponent by keeping his legs wrapped around him, he is said to have the opponent in his guard. The fighter in guard may try to pass the guard for a more offensive positon or to land attacking blows.

REAR NAKED CHOKE

When a fighter has taken another's back, they often wrap one arm around their opponent's neck and apply pressure with the other arms to choke out or force a submission.

HAMMERFIST

Often utilised when in a mounted position, a fighter punches with the bottom of a closed fist, bringing it down as if hammering a nail into wood.

LEG LOCK

Any finishing hold move in which enough pressure is placed on the knee, foot or toes to force an opponent to tap out.

MOUNT

As opposed to being in guard, a mounted position is one in which the fighter on top has his legs around the opponent's body and by controlling him is able to land punches and elbows freely.

SPRAWL AND BRAWL

The process of avoiding takedown attempts from an opponent in order to keep the fight on feet. Developed to counter the dominance of ground and pounders, Chuck Liddell is regarded as one of the masters of this technique.

ARM BAR

An attempt to force an opponent to submit via pressuring an elbow joint by bending it back on itself. Ronda Rousey used this move to defeat nine of her twelve victims.

TAKEDOWN

The action of putting a rival on the floor and mounting them. Coming straight from wrestling, a fighter will either shoot in for a takedown from feet or attempt to throw or trip an opponent to the ground from a clinch.

TAP OUT

When caught in a choke or hold that is in danger of severely damaging a joint or putting you to sleep, fighters submit by tapping the floor or their opponent.

MICHAEL BISPING

Bisping was born on a British military base in Cyprus where his father was stationed, but spent most of his youth in Manchester. He began training in Jiu-Jitsu at the age of eight and proved to be a natural fighter. Still only fifteen, Bisping was already beating grown men in no-holds-barred Knock Down Sport Budo contests.

He went on to win multiple kickboxing titles before briefly quitting martial arts to look for what he called "a real job". But factory work and manual labour was never going to satisfy The Count, and he was soon persuaded back into competition, this time in MMA. Bisping dominated the fledgling British MMA scene for two years and was awarded a place on the UFC's Ultimate Fighter series in 2006.

Bisping won that season of the show and earned a six-figure contract from the UFC. So began a rollercoaster career inside the Octagon which has seen him reach the most fights (27) and most victories (20) in UFC history. His defeats have tended to be hard-fought losses against greats such as Dan Henderson, Rashad Evans, Wanderlei Silva and Vitor Belfort, and it looked like a UFC title would always elude him.

Then in 2016, Bisping defeated the legendary Anderson Silva in London before becoming the first British UFC champion when he claimed the middleweight championship by knocking out Luke Rockhold. He then completed his dream by defending his title, and gaining revenge over Henderson, in an epic battle in front of his own Manchester fans.

NAME:
MICHAEL "THE COUNT" BISPING

FROM:
MANCHESTER, UK

HEIGHT:
6' 1"

MMA RECORD:
31-7

DIVISION:
185LB MIDDLEWEIGHT CHAMPION

BACKGROUND:
KICKBOXING AND JIU-JITSU

CODY GARBRANDT

Born and raised in a small town in rural Ohio, Garbrandt has been fighting since he could walk. Boxing was his first love, but his mother was wary of the heavy blows to the head her son would receive and so pushed Cody and his elder brother Zach towards wrestling. Both excelled, becoming state champions in their respective weight classes.

But the Garbrandt brothers were a wild pair, often settling differences with each other or whoever crossed them with their fists. In an effort to channel his aggression, Cody returned to the boxing gym when he was eighteen and compiled an impressive 32-1 amateur record.

Although he could both wrestle and box to a high standard, a UFC title had always been Garbrandt's dream and he found the motivation he needed to pursue it in 2011 when he met a young cancer sufferer named Maddux Maple. The pair made a pact that Cody would win the world title and Maddux would beat the illness.

Garbrandt has been unstoppable ever since, winning all eleven of his professional MMA fights, nine by way of knockout. Maddux has walked him to the Octagon several times and was there cageside to see his hero outclass the champion Dominic Cruz at UFC 207 in Las Vegas to claim the bantamweight crown and fulfil his side of the pact. Even more incredibly, the brave Maddux is currently winning his fight against cancer and Cody's championship belt has pride of place in his bedroom.

NAME:
CODY "NO LOVE" GARBRANDT

FROM:
OHIO, USA

HEIGHT:
5' 8"

MMA RECORD:
11-0

DIVISION:
135LB BANTAMWEIGHT CHAMPION

BACKGROUND:
WRESTLING AND BOXING

FORREST GRIFFIN V STEPHAN BONNAR TUF 1 FINALE

Griffin v Bonnar I is widely regarded as the fight which saved the UFC. At that time the company was losing money hand over fist and their reality TV show, *The Ultimate Fighter*, was seen as the final role of the dice. In the show, Chuck Liddell and Randy Couture each trained four light heavyweights and four middleweights to take part in a knockout competition. The prize was a six-figure contract with the UFC for the winner and after four months of action, Griffin and Bonnar, faced off in the light heavyweight final.

There was no clear favourite going into the fight. Bonnar had an extensive background in martial arts including Taekwondo, Jiu-Jitsu and Muay Thai. He was also a Golden Gloves boxer and an accomplished high school wrestler. Griffin began boxing and kickboxing before gaining a black belt in Jiu-Jitsu in order to compete effectively in MMA. With so much on the line, both men were determined to leave it all in the Octagon.

ROUND ONE

The opener flew by at a frenetic pace as both fighters appeared happy to throw caution to the wind in the hope of being the first to land a monster punch. Planting their feet and standing in the pocket, it was Griffin who perhaps edged most of the chaotic exchanges. He also managed to land several knees from a Muay Thai clinch. Bonnar was in danger in the final minute as Griffin took his back and tried to lock in a choke, but he squirmed out just before the hooter sounded to pause the action.

ROUND TWO

Near the beginning of the second round, Bonnar faked a kick and then landed a spinning punch. He followed up with a stiff jab directly into Griffin's face before Griffin managed to take his man down. But as the blood flowed freely from the bridge of Forrest's nose, it was clear the jab had done some damage. Griffin kept pounding away at Bonnar on his back, but when they stood up the referee Herb Dean insisted on the cageside doctor inspecting the wound. They went straight back to throwing haymakers after that brief interval and Bonnar rocked Griffin again with a knee. Both men were exhausted as they continued swinging at one another until the bell.

ROUND THREE

Round three was effectively winner takes all and with everyone inside the venue fully aware of what was at stake the atmosphere was electric.

Both warriors were running on empty, but they continued their brutal dance of swinging wild punches at one another and attempting knees from a Muay Thai clinch. It was cruel to declare a winner after such an epic and close-fought battle, but all three judges sided with Griffin by a score of 29-28.

Bonnar was devastated, but Dana White then entered the Octagon to announce that he was also receiving a contract with the UFC. The success of the bout gave the UFC a new lease of life and both fighters went on to enjoy long and successful careers with the company.

QUIZ

There have been 12 different light heavyweight champions in the history of the UFC. Can you work out which eight are disguised in these images? Write your answers in the spaces provided and then check if you're right at the back of the book.

1.

2.

3.

4.

5.

6.

7.

Answers on page 60-61

JOHN KAVANAGH AND THE STRAIGHT BLAST GYM

Conor McGregor's coach, John Kavanagh, was once a professional MMA fighter himself. He was Ireland's first ever black belt in Brazilian Jiu-Jitsu and amassed a respectable 3-3 record in MMA, but somehow he always knew he was better suited to a role in coaching rather than fighting. Kavanagh continues his Jiu-Jitsu training, and was recently awarded his third stripe black belt, but he is now widely regarded as one of the leading coaches working in the UFC today.

Kavanagh established his first gym in Dublin in 2001, and soon became affiliated with Straight Blast Gym International. As its reputation grew, SBG Ireland quickly became the foremost MMA facility in the country. Kavanagh is the head coach overseeing all the training programs, but with MMA being such a multi-disciplined sport he has selected a group of coaches who each specialise in a particular discipline needed to excel in a fight.

In 2009, SBG fighter Tom Egan became the first Irishman to compete inside the Octagon when he fought on the undercard of UFC 93 in Dublin. Though he lost to John Hathaway, it was a huge step forward for the sport within Ireland and a sign that Kavanagh knew what he was doing inside the gym.

Another nine SBG athletes have gone on to join the UFC roster since Egan's debut, including the likes of Cathal Pendred, Patrick Holohan, adopted Irishmen Gunnar Nelson and Artem Lobov, and the first Irishwoman to fight in the UFC, Aisling Daly. Pendred was a champion in Cage Warriors before he made it to the UFC, and they have had other champs like John Phillips in BAMMA, but it is of course Conor McGregor who is the biggest star to emerge from SBG and Kavanagh's tutelage.

PROFILES OF SBG STARS

CATHAL "THE PUNISHER" PENDRED

FROM: Boston, USA

HEIGHT: 6' 1"

MMA RECORD: 17-4-1

DIVISION: 185lbs

BACKGROUND: Jiu-Jitsu

Born in the US but raised in Ireland, Pendred was on a four-fight winning streak inside the Octagon before two quick losses ended his career. He's now focused on a career in Hollywood.

GUNNAR "GUNNI" NELSON

FROM: Reykjavik, Iceland

HEIGHT: 5' 11"

MMA RECORD: 16-3-1

DIVISION: 170lbs

BACKGROUND: Jiu-Jitsu & Karate

Nelson is now regarded as more Irish than Icelandic after a decade living and training in Dublin. He is a UFC veteran with an impressive 7-3 record in the Octagon.

PATRICK "THE HOOLIGAN" HOLOHAN

FROM: Dublin, Ireland

HEIGHT: 5' 9"

MMA RECORD: 12-2-1

DIVISION: 125lbs

BACKGROUND: Jiu-Jitsu

A wildly popular character, Paddy "The Hooligan" Holohan has recently retired with a 3-2 UFC record after winning his final fight in the Octagon in front of his own adoring fans in Dublin.

AISLING "AIS THE BASH" DALY

FROM: Dublin, Ireland

HEIGHT: 5' 3"

MMA RECORD: 16-6

DIVISION: 115lbs

BACKGROUND: Jiu-Jitsu & Muay Thai

Daly was a trailblazer for women's MMA in Ireland. The first professional fighter, she starred in Season 20 of The Ultimate Fighter and fought twice (1-1) in the UFC.

ARTEM "THE RUSSIAN HAMMER" LOBOV

FROM: Nizhny Novgorod, Russia

HEIGHT: 5' 9"

MMA RECORD: 14-13-1, 1 NC

DIVISION: 155lbs

BACKGROUND: Jiu-Jitsu

The second adopted Irishman in the gym, Lobov fought on Team McGregor in Season 22 of The Ultimate Fighter. Currently 2-2 in the Octagon.

DEMETRIOUS JOHNSON

Born in Kentucky but raised in Washington State, Johnson was a stand-out athlete in track and field, cross country running, baseball and wrestling during his youth. But it was the latter discipline that he took most seriously and that in turn led him to mixed martial arts. Watching The Ultimate Fighter inspired him to join a Muay Thai gym and it wasn't long before he was fighting regularly on the amateur MMA circuit. His diminutive size and explosive performances soon earned him the moniker Mighty Mouse.

Johnson took his time mastering the necessary skills before finally turning professional in 2007 and embarking on a ten-fight unbeaten run. He proved his versatility by winning via punches, head kicks, decisions and a variety of submissions including armbars, rear-naked chokes and americanas.

A 14-1 record, his only blemish a decision loss to Brad Pickett, paved the way to a UFC debut and in only his third fight in the Octagon he challenged Dominick Cruz for the bantamweight title. Naturally a much bigger man, Cruz, much like Pickett, proved simply too physically big and strong for Mighty Mouse. But when the UFC created the 125lb flyweight division soon after, Johnson knew he had found a home.

He has remained undefeated ever since, seizing the inaugural flyweight belt in 2012 and successfully defending it ten times to equal the great Anderson Silva's title-defence record. Lightning quick and technically perfect, Johnson is currently the number one ranked pound-for-pound fighter on the planet.

NAME:
DEMETRIOUS "MIGHTY MOUSE" JOHNSON

FROM:
KENTUCKY, USA

HEIGHT:
5' 3"

MMA RECORD:
26-2-1

DIVISION:
125LB FLYWEIGHT CHAMPION

BACKGROUND:
WRESTLING AND MUAY THAI

JOANNA JEDRZEJCZYK

Jedrzejczyk was sixteen years old when she first walked into a Muay Thai gym in her home town of Olsztyn in Poland. At the time she just wanted to lose some weight and feel healthier, but when she won her first tournament just six months later, Joanna knew she was destined for a career in combat sports. For the next ten years, Jedrzejczyk was a major force in the sport of Muay Thai, becoming a five-time world amateur champion and a four-time European champion.

By 2012 she had a college degree in physical education and was considering a career in teaching when she was offered the chance to try MMA. Two amateur and six professional contests later, JJ was invited to join the UFC roster and any thoughts of becoming a teacher were put on hold.

Her rise through the strawweight division has been meteoric. Although her striking skills were initially raw, she punched with such speed, quantity and ferocity that she soon became the most feared women at 115lbs. In just her third fight in the Octagon, Jedrzejczyk overpowered Carla Esparza in Texas to wrench away the champion's crown inside two rounds.

She has since defended her title in Berlin, Melbourne, Las Vegas, New York and Dallas with a series of dominant performances. Along the way, JJ has mastered the sprawl and brawl defence and refined her striking prowess. The victories and improvements have earned her the number one ranking in the UFC's pound-for-pound list.

NAME:
JOANNA "JJ" JEDRZEJCZYK

FROM:
OLSZTYN, POLAND

HEIGHT:
5' 6"

MMA RECORD:
14-0

DIVISION:
115LB STRAWWEIGHT CHAMPION

BACKGROUND:
MUAY THAI AND BOXING

CHUCK LIDDELL

The Iceman Chuck Liddell was for a long time the face of the UFC franchise and is widely credited with driving the popularity of MMA to a mainstream audience. He is also one of the best light heavyweight fighters to ever grace the Octagon.

Liddell's grandfather introduced him to combat sports when he taught a young Chuck and his brothers some rudimentary boxing stances and punches. He then took up Koei-Kan karate at the age of twelve, before going on to become a NCAA Division 1 wrestler in college. Liddell soon added kickboxing to his arsenal, compiling a 22-2 amateur record, and when MMA caught his attention he supplemented his ever-growing skillset with Jiu-Jitsu.

By the time he made his MMA debut at UFC 17 in 1998, Chuck was close to being a complete fighter. He proved this with the variety of his attacks and the numerous ways in which he could win a fight. A knockout by head kick, a knockout with punches, a rear-naked choke submission and a controlled unanimous decision were all present amongst his first seven victories.

During this time he also became famous for perfecting a technique known as *sprawl and brawl* which effectively combatted the

ground and pound approach then dominant in MMA. It was a way to fend off takedown attempts and keep the fight on the feet where the better punchers and kickers had the upper hand.

Liddell's mastery of this new technique ultimately proved decisive in his historic trilogy with his great rival, Randy Couture. Couture won their first bout at UFC 43 by taking Liddell down and wearing him out on the floor, but The Iceman gained revenge in spectacular fashion two years later when he knocked Couture out midway through the opening round at UFC 52. It was set up perfectly for a decider and the pair broke all viewing records when they clashed at UFC 57 in Vegas, Liddell again victorious via a devastating KO in the second round.

The two other great rivals during Liddell's career were Tito Ortiz and Wanderlei Silva. Once a training partner and friend of Ortiz,

the relationship had soured by the time Chuck knocked him out at the beginning of the second round with a ferocious onslaught at UFC 47. Their rematch at UFC 66, another stoppage victory for Liddell, was the first UFC contest to sell more than one million PPVs. The rivalry with Silva built from afar when the Brazilian was the Pride champion in Japan. When they finally met in the Octagon, Liddell was awarded the decision after a classic encounter.

But The Iceman was already on the slide by then, having lost his title to Quinton Jackson earlier in the year. Inducted into the Hall of Fame in 2009, Liddell is now a familiar face on TV and the big screen having appeared in the likes of Dancing with the Stars, Bones and the movie Kick-Ass 2.

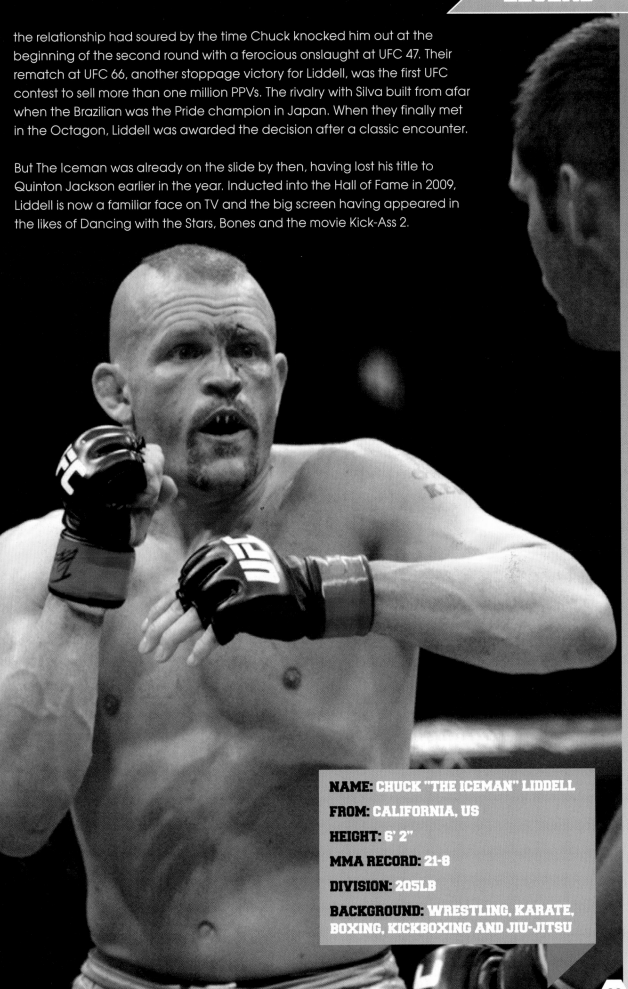

NAME: CHUCK "THE ICEMAN" LIDDELL

FROM: CALIFORNIA, US

HEIGHT: 6' 2"

MMA RECORD: 21-8

DIVISION: 205LB

BACKGROUND: WRESTLING, KARATE, BOXING, KICKBOXING AND JIU-JITSU

CONOR MCGREGOR'S EXTRAVAGANT LIFESTYLE

Conor McGregor may now be a famous multi-millionaire, but it wasn't so long ago he was an apprentice plumber in Dublin who needed to cash a benefits cheque to fund his fledgling MMA career. Having risen from such humble beginnings, it is no surprise that the UFC superstar is now determined to enjoy every penny of his hard-earned wealth.

His first car may have been a bottom of the range Vauxhall Astra, but McGregor is now steadily amassing a fleet of some of the finest wheels on the planet. He already has a £150k Bentley, a £300k Lamborghini and a £400k Rolls Royce in his garage and it won't be long before he has a different super-car for every day of the week.

With every training session and fight spent in a non-descript pair of Lycra shorts, Conor likes to dress up for every other occasion. With his tailor-made suits by Gucci or Dolce & Gabbana, he has become a fashion icon, even gracing the front cover of GQ Style magazine.

And when it is time for a major press conference, expect the Irishman to make the grandest of entrances in a lavish fur coat and expensive sunglasses. Then watch closely as he raises his hand, lets his sleeve slip up a few inches, and reveals a gold Rolex watch the size of a fist.

When it is time to go home, Conor now simply boards a private jet with a holdall full of cash to spend when he lands. And with more mega fights to come in 2018, McGregor's net worth, and with it his lavish lifestyle, is only going to grow.

CONOR MCGREGOR V NATE DIAZ II UFC 202

Conor "Notorious" McGregor and Nate Diaz first met at UFC 196 in March of 2016 when the American brought the Irishman's fifteen-fight winning streak to an end with a rear-naked choke in round two. McGregor, the 145lb featherweight champ, had originally been training for a 155lb lightweight contest against Rafael dos Anjos and many put the defeat down to the physical advantages of the naturally bigger Diaz and the fight taking place at 170lbs.

Nevertheless, when McGregor immediately sought revenge he insisted upon a rematch at the exact same weight in which he had lost the first time around. The UFC was only too happy to oblige and the date was set for UFC 202 in Las Vegas, a mere five months on from their initial dance in the Octagon.

ROUND ONE

It was a different Conor McGregor that emerged in round one, a fighter in a Zen-like state of calm. Conscious that the extra weight had badly hurt his cardio fitness in the first fight, Notorious was extremely measured in his attacks, prioritising accuracy and efficiency of movement over power. He brutalised Diaz's leading leg with a series of kicks before sending Nate to the canvas with an overhand right. Rather than jump all over his stricken foe, McGregor simply gestured for Diaz to get back on his feet so he could receive more of the same punishment.

ROUND TWO

It was McGregor's deadly left hand which did the damage in the opening half of the second round as that fist twice dropped Diaz to the floor. With the vicious kicks still crashing into the American's thigh and causing his legs to buckle dramatically, it seemed like the end was near for Nate. But once more McGregor's endurance suddenly seemed to lag and Nate bounced, ending the round on the offensive with an onslaught of punches against the cage fence.

ROUND THREE

Round three belonged to Diaz as McGregor's tank continued to empty. As Notorious looked at the clock and attempted to circle away from trouble at every opportunity, Diaz landed a series of heavy blows and even laughed at one point, clearly expecting a repeat of the first encounter. But despite unrelenting pressure, McGregor managed to stay on his feet and survive the storm.

ROUND FOUR

Incredibly, McGregor caught a second wind on his stool between rounds and emerged for the fourth with renewed vigour. He targeted Diaz's thighs and calves again with stinging kicks and then opened up with punches and elbows to leave his opponent bloodied and on the retreat. Diaz responded with an attempted takedown, but McGregor easily fended it off and then landed more lefts and rights to Nate's battered face to guarantee him the round.

ROUND FIVE

The ebb and flow continued in the last. McGregor began on the front foot but Diaz rallied and punished the Irishman with elbows against the cage. Finally, after almost twenty-five minutes of trying, Nate managed to take Conor down cleanly but it was too little too late and McGregor was declared a majority decision winner by scores of 48-47, 47-47 and 48-47.

TYRON WOODLEY

The eleventh of thirteen children, Woodley is another UFC fighter who starred in a variety of sports throughout school and college. American football and wrestling were Tyron's specialities and the latter earned him a scholarship to an NCAA Division 1 university from which he graduated with a degree in agricultural economics.

When he noticed that athletes from a wrestling background were performing well in the mixed martial arts arena, Woodley walked into an MMA gym and asked to be given a spot on the undercard of an upcoming amateur show. He won his debut inside twenty seconds and soon boasted a 7-0 record. He narrowly missed out on a spot in The Ultimate Fighter's season nine, but his performances in the trials convinced him it was the time to turn pro.

After testing the water on a couple of small shows, Woodley signed for the Strikeforce promotional banner and won his first eight fights. He lost his tenth to Nate Marquardt for the welterweight title, but was still welcomed into the UFC the following year.

The Chosen One lost two of his first five inside the Octagon, but wins over names like Josh Koscheck and Carlos Condit ensured his position with the company was safe. Three fights later, Woodley knocked out the champion Robbie Lawler with a thunderous overhand right to claim the UFC welterweight championship. His reign thus far has consisted of two epic battles with Stephen "Wonderboy" Thompson, the first declared a draw and the second a unanimous decision victory for Tyron.

NAME:
TYRON "THE CHOSEN ONE" WOODLEY

FROM:
MISSOURI, US

HEIGHT:
5' 9"

MMA RECORD:
16-3-1

DIVISION:
170LB WELTERWEIGHT CHAMPION

BACKGROUND:
WRESTLING AND JIU-JITSU

CRISTIANE JUSTINO

Cris Cyborg hails from Curitiba, the mixed martial arts capital of Brazil, but she was actually a professional handball player before she became a fighter. It was only when she realised her natural aggression would be better served in a ring or Octagon where there is no possibility of a red card that she fully focused on the martial arts.

Cyborg is a brown belt in Brazilian Jiu-Jitsu and has won several international grappling competitions. She is also a black kruang in Muay Thai with a winning professional record in that discipline of fighting. But it is in the world of MMA that she has truly excelled and become one of the most feared fighters on the planet.

After losing via a kneebar submission in her debut in 2005, Cyborg has gone on a twelve-year, nineteen-fight unbeaten streak. Along the way she has picked up world titles in Strikeforce, Invicta FC and the UFC. She was also the first female to headline a major MMA event when she destroyed the unbeaten American star Gina Carano to claim the inaugural Strikeforce featherweight championship.

A ferocious attacker with both fist and knee, Cyborg has stopped sixteen of her victims and it is almost a decade since someone took her the distance. Often regarded as one of the most avoided fighters in MMA, Cyborg is now the UFC's 145lb champion and is ready to take on all-comers.

NAME:
CRISTIANE "CRIS CYBORG" JUSTINO

FROM:
CURITIBA, BRAZIL

HEIGHT:
5' 8"

MMA RECORD:
18-1 - 1 NC

DIVISION:
145LB FEATHERWEIGHT CHAMPION

BACKGROUND:
MUAY THAI, JIU-JITSU, BOXING AND WRESTLING

RONDA ROUSEY

Rowdy Ronda Rousey became the UFC's first female fighter in 2012 and by the beginning of 2015 she was widely regarded as the most dominant athlete, male or female, in professional sports. In appealing to demographics previously unreachable by fighters, Rousey transcended MMA and grew into a truly global superstar and a hero to millions.

It all began in Riverside, California, when her mother, herself a decorated Judoka, began training her eleven-year-old daughter. Ronda was a natural and when she accidentally broke her mother's wrist in one session a couple of years later, both knew that Judo was the sport for her. Rousey's list of honours in Judo is almost endless, culminating with a bronze medal at the 2008 Athens Olympics.

After working a few dead-end jobs when she returned from Greece, Ronda decided she could never settle in a regular job. Looking for a profession to excite her, she opted for MMA and began training in Muay Thai and Jiu-Jitsu to build on her Judo base. She began her amateur career in 2006 and submitted her first three opponents using an armbar in a combined 104 seconds.

Her first four professional opponents barely lasted longer, all succumbing to Rousey's fearsome armbar inside the opening minute. The Strikeforce champion, Miesha Tate, lasted a few minutes longer, but the result was the same as Ronda claimed her first pro title. That victory also caught the attention of UFC President Dana White and led to Rowdy being announced as the UFC's first female fighter and original bantamweight champion less than a year later.

Inside the Octagon, Rousey continued her triumphant blaze of destruction. A rematch with Tate made it into the third, but five other challengers were decimated in the opening round. It was a dominance never seen before in MMA. White called her the greatest

athlete he has ever worked with and likened her performances to a young Mike Tyson destroying the heavyweight boxing division in the 1980s.

She was now one of the most famous women on the planet: a Hollywood actress, a best-selling author, and a regular on chat shows and magazine covers. Little girls were begging their mothers to dress them as Ronda for parties and the mums were only too happy

NAME: "ROWDY" RONDA ROUSEY

FROM: CALIFORNIA, US

HEIGHT: 5' 7"

MMA RECORD: 12-2

DIVISION: 135LB

BACKGROUND: JUDO

to oblige. She brought millions of fans to the UFC that would otherwise never have given MMA a second's thought.

It was therefore a major shock when the fairy tale was rudely interrupted by the excellent stand-up boxing skills of Holly Holm at UFC 193. Rousey returned a year later but was blown away by new champion Amanda Nunes inside a minute. Nevertheless, whether or not we see her in the Octagon again, Ronda's status as the most popular and the greatest female UFC fighter ever remains undiminished.

SPOT THE DIFFERENCE

Can you spot the 8 differences in these images?

Answers on page 60-61

49

ANDERSON SILVA V

CHAEL SONNEN UFC 117

By 2010, the great Anderson "The Spider" Silva was eleven fights into his unbeaten streak in the UFC and many believed he couldn't be defeated. But the Brazilian was also receiving criticism for the manner of some of his victories, particularly the recent unanimous decision over Demian Maia when Silva was content to humiliate his opponent without ever attempting to finish the contest. UFC President Dana White walked away from the fight before the end, declaring it an embarrassment.

So in an effort to reignite The Spider's killer instinct in the Octagon, the UFC turned to Chael Sonnen. Sonnen was a NCAA Division 1 wrestler before adding Jiu-Jitsu to his game and entering the world of MMA. He was on a three-fight winning streak at the time, but more importantly he was known as the brashest trash-talker in the sport. If anyone could get under the champion's skin and force him to fight aggressively again it would be Sonnen and the American did his best with jibes about Silva's pedigree, his country and even his choice of clothing in the build-up.

When they finally faced one another inside the Octagon at UFC 117 in California on 7 August 2010, they produced a fight regarded as one of the most dramatic in MMA history.

ROUND ONE

Sonnen started as he meant to go on, forcing the pace with constant pressure. He rocked the champ with a couple of left hands and after a series of punches he shot and took Silva down. From there he landed multiple times to earn the first round.

ROUND TWO

The Spider tried some leg kicks but Chael caught one and took his man down. Silva held on tight but could do nothing to prevent his ears being boxed and head slammed off the canvas. The champion attempted an armbar, but repeatedly ate elbows and fists to lose another round.

ROUND THREE

The third followed a similar pattern. Anderson tried to be more aggressive at the outset, but was soon on his back, struggling to survive under the weight of Sonnen and his punches for the full five minutes.

ROUND FOUR

The beginning of the fourth was the first time Silva had any real success as he landed several vicious kicks and rocked Sonnen with a punch. He then sprawled to defend a takedown and briefly held top position before the challenger reversed it and resumed his ground and pound dominance. Silva opened a gash above Sonnen's left eye with an elbow from the bottom, but it was still the American's round.

ROUND FIVE

The champ clearly needed a stoppage to retain his title and it looked unlikely when he once more found himself on the canvas, with Sonnen in side control attempting a choke. But as time was running out and Silva was still on his back defending against the punches raining down on him, he sensationally locked in a triangle and forced the submission. With less than two minutes remaining, The Spider had grabbed an incredible victory from the jaws of certain defeat.

BROCK LESNAR

Brock Lesnar grew up on a dairy farm in South Dakota and was an impressive and powerful athlete from a very young age. Wrestling and American football were his two specialities, but by the time he attended college his focus was fully on the former. He was the NCAA Division 1 heavyweight champion in 2000 and finished his distinguished college wrestling career with an enviable 106-5 record.

Lesnar was signed by the World Wrestling Federation (now the WWE) and would go on to become one of the biggest names in professional wrestling. He had one further pit-stop, a try-out for the Minnesota Vikings NFL team in 2004, before the heavyweight champion of the scripted sports entertainment world entered the very real and totally unscripted mixed martial arts arena.

The big man cut his teeth in a K-1 match-up which saw him overpower his opponent with punches in a little over a minute. That was all it took for the UFC to accept there was fighting substance behind the larger-than-life character and offer Lesnar an opportunity against Octagon legend Frank Mir at UFC 81. Mir, an eleven-fight UFC veteran and former champion, had too much experience that night and submitted Brock in the opening round, but such was the buzz around Lesnar in the Octagon that he was guaranteed to be invited back.

He returned with a win a few months later at UFC 87 and then blasted the great Randy Couture out inside two rounds to become the UFC heavyweight champion at UFC 91. He defended that title twice, and gained sweet revenge over Mir in doing so, before being stopped by Cain Velasquez at UFC 121 in California. By now he was the biggest PPV attraction that MMA had ever seen, and would remain so until Conor McGregor swaggered into town five years later.

Brock returned to the WWE and continued to be the biggest draw in wrestling as he became a five-time champion and enjoyed high-profile feuds with the likes of The Undertaker, Randy Orton and Goldberg. But he always found it difficult to resist the lure of genuine combat and was twice more tempted to test himself against the heavyweight division's best in the Octagon.

Brock Lesnar may not have been the most accomplished mixed martial artist nor the most decorated UFC fighter, but he held an aura that captivated fans and is the only example of a crossover star from professional wrestling. He is now forty years of age, but rumours of one last fight in the Octagon, potentially against the seemingly untouchable Jon Jones, continue to do the rounds. It remains to be seen whether Dana White can make that bout a reality, but MMA fans are certainly praying they get another chance to see the big man in action.

NAME: BROCK LESNAR

FROM: SOUTH DAKOTA, US

HEIGHT: 6' 3"

MMA RECORD: 5-3 - 1 NC

DIVISION: HEAVYWEIGHT

BACKGROUND: WRESTLING

MAX HOLLOWAY

Holloway found his way into the martial arts in his mid-teens when he followed his friend into a kickboxing gym on the Hawaiian island of Oahu. The trainer watched him hitting the speed bag and immediately knew that Max was a gifted fighter. He soon added Muay Thai and Jiu-Jitsu to his skillset and started competing on the local amateur MMA circuit.

By the age of eighteen, Holloway was already fighting as a professional and the MMA world regarded him as something of a prodigy. He confirmed his pedigree when he beat the experienced Harris Sarmiento to claim the X-1 lightweight championship in Honolulu.

Unable to ignore his talent any longer, the UFC came knocking and made Holloway the youngest fighter on their roster when he took on Dustin Poirier at the tender age of twenty. Twelve-fight veteran Poirier proved a step up too soon and Max would lose two more of his first six outings, including a defeat to Conor McGregor. But his youth and potential ensured the UFC were happy to give him another shot and Max hasn't looked back since.

He stopped his next four opponents, then moved up in class again to claim the scalps of Cole Miller and Cub Swanson. When he bludgeoned Anthony Pettis to a standstill to make it ten victories in a row, it was clear Holloway was ready for a title shot. He seized the featherweight crown in spectacular style by stopping the great Brazilian Jose Aldo in Rio de Janeiro at UFC 212.

NAME:
MAX "BLESSED" HOLLOWAY

FROM:
HAWAII, US

HEIGHT:
5' 11"

MMA RECORD:
18-3

DIVISION:
145LB FEATHERWEIGHT CHAMPION

BACKGROUND:
KICKBOXING, MUAY THAI AND JIU-JITSU

JON JONES

It all started for Jon "Bones" Jones, a top high-school wrestler and college American football player, when he dropped out of university and into an MMA gym to earn money to support his pregnant girlfriend. After six victories in his first three months as a professional, the UFC came calling and the rest is history.

Jones has combined elite-level striking and grappling with natural physical gifts and an almost supernatural athletic ability to dominate every opponent he has faced in the Octagon. In his twenty-four fights over a ten-year career he is yet to truly be troubled, the only blemish on his record a disqualification against Matt Hamill for illegal use of the elbow.

Legendary names such as Quinton Jackson, Rashad Evans, Chael Sonnen, Lyoto Machida and Daniel Cormier have all fallen well short in their attempts to dethrone the champ since he first claimed the 205lb title by stopping Shogun Rua at UFC 128 to become the youngest ever titleholder.

Along the way, Jones has broken the record for the most light heavyweight defences and the most knockouts. He is also one of only two men to submit multiple opponents on their feet.

Jon Jones may well be the greatest mixed martial artist to ever step foot in the Octagon. Now back as the light heavyweight champion and the pound-for-pound king, he intends to go unbeaten for the rest of his career. It will certainly take someone very special to deny him.

NAME: JON "BONES" JONES

FROM: NEW YORK, USA

HEIGHT: 6' 4"

MMA RECORD: 23-1

DIVISION: 205LB LIGHT HEAVYWEIGHT CHAMPION

BACKGROUND: WRESTLING, JIU-JITSU, MUAY THAI AND GAIDOJUTSU

THE FIGHT OF THE CENTURY

In the summer of 2015, Conor McGregor wasn't even a champion in the UFC yet. Floyd Mayweather, meanwhile, had just beaten Manny Pacquiao in the richest, and one of the most anti-climactic, boxing matches in history. McGregor was preparing to face Chad Mendes when he was invited onto the Conan O'Brien show where the host raised the possibility of fighting Mayweather.

. "Who would not like to dance around the ring for $180m?" Conor joked in reference to the cheque Floyd had just received for an easy night's work against Pacquiao. But then he got serious. "I would step into his world and I would box him if the opportunity arose." Before finally adding "I would most certainly dismantle him also."

The entire boxing world, and a lot of the MMA world, scoffed. An MMA fighter without a title taking on one of the greatest boxers of his generation in a boxing ring? It was absurd, everyone said. Nothing more than a cheap publicity stunt. Only two men truly believed it would happen: Conor "Notorious" McGregor and Floyd "Money" Mayweather.

Conor had lit a fire under Floyd with his mocking comments and it wasn't long before the unbeaten boxer responded. For over a year they traded barbs on social media, Mayweather flaunting his superior wealth while McGregor teased back that he was the biggest draw in combat sports.

While Mayweather sat at home retired with his perfect 49-0 record, Conor kept fighting in the Octagon. He beat Chad Mendes then knocked Jose Aldo out to claim the featherweight belt. He lost to Diaz, then gained his revenge, before beating Eddie Alvarez to add the lightweight strap to his collection. He appeared unstoppable in the MMA world, but then he applied for and was awarded a boxing licence.

By early 2017, it looked like the fantasy fight was becoming a reality. Offers and counter offers were made and laughed at. Dana White and John Kavanagh declared they expected the bout to happen while Floyd announced he was out of retirement. Finally, on 15 June, it was confirmed: Mayweather versus McGregor on 26 August in Las Vegas.

The press tour was like nothing the sporting world had ever seen before. Four cities in three countries in four nights, with over 50,000 fans attending just to watch the combatants speak. When that was finished the two men locked themselves in their respective gyms to prepare. For Mayweather it was a simple matter of following the winning formula he has been using his entire boxing life. But it was something new for McGregor who hadn't boxed competitively since he was a young teen in Dublin.

The Irishman kept his usual team around him, but he did bring in the occasional outsider from the boxing world like referee Joe Cortez and the former two-weight world champion Paulie Malignaggi. The relationship with Malignaggi ended acrimoniously when footage emerged of the boxer taking a beating from the MMA fighter. It all built the suspense and left the world holding its breath in anticipation of exactly how the Notorious would try to defeat Money May.

Las Vegas was Irish for a weekend as the Strip was painted green, white and gold by McGregor's legion of fans. All truly believed

he could once again do the impossible, but it wasn't to be this time. The UFC champ began well and was ahead on the scorecards early on, but the old master boxer Mayweather had too much experience inside the ring. Conor battled bravely, performing better and lasting longer than anyone outside MMA thought he could, until the ref waved it off in the tenth round. He lost the fight, but McGregor won the respect of his opponent and the boxing fraternity. He also swaggered out of the arena substantially richer!

QUIZ AND PUZZLE ANSWERS

P14-15 - FAMOUS FANS

1. Mike Tyson
2. Gordon Ramsay
3. Arnold Schwarzenegger
4. Shaq O'Neal
5. Odell Beckham Jr.
6. Kanye West
7. Snoop Dogg
8. Niall Horan
9. Mel Gibson
10. Hugh Jackman
11. Ben Affleck
12. Paris Hilton
13. Donald Trump
14. Zac Efron
15. Will Smith
16. Justin Timberlake
17. Charlize Theron
18. Mark Wahlberg

P16 - WORDSEARCH

F	N	G	R	O	U	N	D	A	N	D	P	O	U	N	D	R
G	B	S	P	R	A	W	L	A	N	D	B	R	A	W	L	N
K	L	O	C	T	A	G	O	N	Z	V	V	K	N	T	F	O
J	J	G	X	W	C	M	T	H	P	X	V	C	N	K	Y	I
I	B	E	R	B	Z	K	R	T	X	T	R	M	R	Z	G	T
U	L	T	D	V	N	M	S	N	L	E	X	W	V	X	Y	A
J	J	L	Y	R	P	A	M	U	D	C	R	Z	Y	T	C	R
I	K	J	L	T	Z	Q	M	I	B	E	G	D	N	T	T	K
T	J	D	V	J	J	E	P	O	S	M	W	H	B	G	N	N
S	Z	K	Y	K	M	S	J	T	R	O	I	M	M	T	N	A
U	G	C	T	Y	E	W	L	C	R	O	T	S	D	K	R	P
N	K	D	N	H	K	I	T	J	Z	B	C	H	S	T	M	Y
A	B	V	T	W	N	F	C	Y	V	V	T	E	T	I	Q	K
M	X	M	J	G	R	W	X	Q	V	T	K	B	R	V	O	P
E	V	M	C	R	L	N	X	L	L	X	W	J	X	G	M	N
C	T	P	M	L	I	A	H	T	Y	A	U	M	J	K	H	P
I	R	E	T	H	G	I	F	E	T	A	M	I	T	L	U	F

P32 - QUIZ

1. Jon Jones
2. Frank Shamrock
3. Tito Ortiz
4. Randy Couture
5. Quinton Jackson
6. Rashad Evans
7. Chuck Liddell

P24 - CROSSWORD

```
              ¹F        ²F E R T I T T A ³A
   ⁴C      ⁵W H I T E⁶                  A
   A        L      H        ⁷G R A C I E  E
   R        O      I                      K
   L      ⁸B O     R        ⁹H            W
   A        N      T   ¹⁰N O T O R I O U S O
   E        E      E        L            N
   S        S      ¹¹C O L O R A D O      O
   P              E        Y
   A                        H
   ¹²R E A R N A K E D C H O K E
   Z                        L
   A                   ¹³A R M B A R
              T
   ¹⁴A N D E R S O N S I L V A
```

P48-49 - SPOT THE DIFFERENCE

61